WIGANOSOPHY

WIGANOSOPHY

WHAT IT MEANS TO BE A WIGAN WARRIORS FAN

MATT MACAULAY

Matador
9 Priory Business Park,
Wistow Road, Kibworth Beauchamp,
Leicestershire. LE8 0RX
Tel: 0116 279 2299
Email: books@troubador.co.uk
Web: www.troubador.co.uk/matador
Twitter: @matadorbooks

ISBN 978 1784625 108

British Library Cataloguing in Publication Data.
A catalogue record for this book is available from the British Library.

Printed and bound in the UK by TJ International, Padstow, Cornwall
Typeset in 11pt Aldine401 BT by Troubador Publishing Ltd, Leicester, UK

Matador is an imprint of Troubador Publishing Ltd

This book is dedicated to all "number eighteens", wherever they may be. To those faithful devotees of the club who endure the highs, the lows and the swings and roundabouts of outrageous sporting fortune while following the Warriors.

Mostly, though, it is dedicated to my wife, Sarah, who has to endure me while I'm enduring the highs, the lows and the swings and roundabouts of outrageous sporting fortune while following the Warriors.

CONTENTS

THE BIG QUESTIONS

Philosophy is all about the big questions. You know the ones – the scary questions that give people the willies. They keep people awake at night. They prey on your mind and loiter with intent in the dingier corners of your subconscious self. Yes, those questions. The ultimate questions. The questions regarding life, the universe and everything. Deep, profound questions such as:

Why are we here? Is there a god? What is the meaning of life? What happens when we die? What is reality?

and

Is there life in Leigh?

Wiganosophy is just another branch of philosophical thought. Like philosophy, Wiganosophy is also about big questions, but while your average philosopher will be splashing about in the shallow end with questions about the problem of evil and suffering, the Wiganosopher

1

will be getting to grips with far more important matters. Wiganosophy, you see, is about those big questions on the most crucial topic of all. It is about being a devotee of Wigan Warriors Rugby League Football Club. By comparison, matters of life and death seem almost trivial.

The biggest questions of all for the Wiganosopher are those about identity and belonging, and it is here where we shall start. While Rene Descartes began his philosophical musings with the question of his own existence, any Wiganosopher worth his or her salt would begin with a question like, "why am I a Wigan supporter?"

Descartes was working on the hunch that he did actually exist. To be fair, we've all had that hunch at some point in our lives. But Descartes was a bit worried that he might not exist. He suspected that he was just being tricked by a wicked demon into thinking he existed. So he spent a whole day talking to his stove before coming up with his now legendary answer – "I think therefore I am".[1]

The Wiganosophy equivalent is to be a fan who is almost entirely convinced that Wigan Warriors RLFC is the best team in the world, but is having niggling doubts whispered into his head by wicked St Helens supporters.

---

[1] Descartes took full credit for this and never divulged exactly how much of the intellectual input had actually come from the stove itself. My own personal thoughts are that Descartes' conclusion is largely the work of the stove, on the basis that a man who talks to stoves is probably a nutter and as such is never going to come up with anything important.

Probably on internet message boards, where they feel safest.

As supporters of teams, we want to know that we are supporting the right one – that there is something special and worthy about it. This is why the question of identity and belonging is so important. It gives meaning, depth and purpose to the time we spend watching our team.

For the Wiganosopher, the question of identity and belonging itself is probably best split into two separate parts:

1. Why Wigan? Or, to put it another way, is there anything particularly special or important about the town of Wigan?
2. Why rugby league? Is there any philosophical, ethical or moral reason why the sport of rugby league is worthy of devotion?

The first question pertains to the town itself. Why would somebody feel any form of attachment to a place like Wigan? Once that question has been satisfactorily answered, the second question can be tackled from a position of strength. Only when light has been thrown upon the answers to both questions can you begin to understand why Wigan Warriors Rugby League Football Club is so worthy of your time, energy and support.

QUESTION ONE: IS WIGAN SPECIAL?

So let's start with that first important question – "Why Wigan?"

For most people, on one level, the answer is probably quite simple.

"Why are you so fond of Wigan?" you might ask those quite simple people.

"Easy," they might reply, "I live here."

That's fair enough. You can't argue with that sort of logic. It is quite understandable that many people feel attached to the town because they live in it. Or because they were born in it. These are two perfectly acceptable reasons for anybody to feel a sense of affection for Wigan. However, like the miners of yesteryear, I want to dig a little deeper into Wigan. It is my supposition that there is something about the town that fosters a dangerously high level of attachment even for people who don't fall into those categories.

I love Wigan.

There, I've said it. And I don't feel dirty (but I am blushing a little bit).

I'm not sure why or how, but I love the place. I am the first to admit that, by rights, I should have no real claim to be a lover of this town. I do not live in Wigan and I wasn't born in Wigan. And yet there is definitely love there, of a sort, for this solid, northern mill and mining town.

It is true that I did once live in the borough of Wigan – in Hindley, to be precise. I lived there for about five years, which isn't a particularly long time. You wouldn't have thought it would be long enough to form a lasting attachment, especially as it was all such a long time ago. But here I am, forty years later, attached.

Curiously, I find great difficulty in even trying to describe my love for Wigan; it's like I know that the feeling is there but I'm not entirely sure of what it is. I suppose the thing it is most like is the sort of affection you continue to feel towards a childhood sweetheart, years after you've gone your separate ways.

Wigan was my first girlfriend.

The one who I never really fancied to start with, but we ended up holding hands a lot because…well, because there wasn't much choice around. To be honest, I felt I could do better. That's why I left her. And years later, even after we've both had a string of other partners, we keep being drawn together. I keep a little flame burning for her. I keep an eye on her Facebook updates. I find a lot of reasons to drive past the place where she lives. And when I see those wonderful words on that sign – "Welcome to Wigan!"[2] my heart does a little leap while my brain looks on with unguarded suspicion.

My brain is right to be suspicious. After all, this is Wigan we're talking about.

---

2   That is assuming the words haven't been removed for fear of offending Wigan Athletic supporters.

Warning – I am now going to be brutally honest. Brace yourself and sit down if necessary because this might hurt a little bit.

There is nothing immediately special about this town or its people. Not upon first glance, anyway. I've lived in enough cities, towns and villages to know that wherever people live there are incidents of breathtaking selflessness and of heartbreaking callousness. There are heroes and villains and all the people in-between who are at once more heroic and more villainous than those who manage to achieve fame or notoriety. This is the case in every town, and Wigan is no exception. Yes, Wigan has its fair share of sights and areas of outstanding beauty. But it certainly has no more than its fair share. And to be honest, I've seen better. In Britain alone I have encountered far more glorious and beautiful sights. I have crossed the highlands of Scotland by canoe, I have scaled the mountains of North Wales, the Lake District and Scotland. I've explored the contrasting moods of the White and Dark Peak Districts. I've sat on the beaches of Aberdeen and Abersoch. I've looked on in awe as I saw the sun rise out of the sea like a burning angel and I've seen that same celestial body infuse the ocean with golden warmth as it sank from sight off the coast of Wales. I've seen the rain sparkle and glitter as it bounces off the neon lights of Leicester Square.

And I've seen an old lady having a wee in a shop doorway in Library Street, Wigan.

You'll find no Cherry And White tinted spectacles

here. I see Wigan for what it is and nothing else. It is a sizeable northern mill and mining town that has suffered as much as any other, but that has always managed to bounce back. Wigan boasts an impressive history and it bears the scars of its impressive history. It ain't no looker, but it's a town with a heart. It's got my heart, for one. It has always had it. It is the birthplace of my earliest coherent memories – the town where I spent my formative years and, for me, the place that fostered my initial feelings of family and security.

But I'm a fickle beast and having spent the larger part of my childhood in Liverpool, and with the influence of my mother's side of the family who were from Warrington via Widnes (and theirs has always been an inestimable influence – God, how I love them!), well, I could just as well have been a Saint or a Wire or a Chemic.

Fortunately, that's not how things turned out, and there are probably some very good reasons why I have never felt the urge to follow those lesser teams.

There is a feeling I get sometimes when I think of my youth; a wave of nostalgia that catches me and carries me along for a few meagre seconds. It is fleeting, yet it has such potency that I am continually enthralled by it. The best way to describe it is as "a heady amalgamation of the essence of my childhood." Actually, there are probably better ways, but I can't think of any at the moment. It is revealing, though, that so many of these childhood memories are centred around the experience of being at rugby games.

The cold, harsh, bracing wind battering against my coat; a warming Styrofoam cup of watery hot chocolate and the pungent smells of the Douglas Stand. The bright, clean, dazzling colours of cherry red and white shirts spilling out onto the pitch to the tune that I once foolishly described as "clown music" (*"It's the Entrance of t'Gladiators, lad – and don't you forget it!"*). I didn't forget it. I liked the idea of gladiators and that piece of music inspires me to this very day. As does the sight of players soaked in the combination of mud and rainwater that was known to us as "slutch". The Central Park scoreboard. Henderson Gill's greasy legs. The names of many other players are there too, nestling in my happier memories. Brian Case, Martin Foy, Nicky Kiss, Gary Stephenson, Danny Campbell, Jinking Jimmy Fairhurst, Colin Whitfield (whose brother was "the invisible referee *we could never see*").

I remember having to memorise and recant the names of the entire first team before I was bought my first Wigan scarf. I loved that scarf – it was a real, proper official Wigan Rugby League scarf. I convinced myself that the red was "cherrier" than that of any other red and white scarf you could purchase anywhere else. That's what made it stand out as a true Wigan scarf. As far as I was concerned, as I walked down streets of towns as far away as Newquay and Bognor (yes, I wore it on my holidays in the height of summer – which meant that my head also glowed cherry red against the white of the rest of my body) the people passing me would see me and recognise it instantly, thinking "Oh look – a Wigan scarf!"

In reality they were probably just thinking "Oh look – a sweaty freak!"

Ah yes, it all comes back to me so vividly when the memory takes me.

Mostly though, above all else, those few seconds of nostalgia remind me of the bond I found with my father as we travelled to and experienced those games side by side. Win or lose hardly mattered in those early days, what mattered was that I was with him. There was no guardedness between us at the match, none of the affectation of an adult with an agenda saying the things that adults are meant to say to children. It was just me and him experiencing the game in an atmosphere of total candour. This is how we first came to understand each other – we were Wiganers.

It is something I always bear in mind when talking to supporters of other teams. Geographical placement is only one small aspect of fandom. The rest is embedded within family ties and relationships that have unshakeable foundations. From the father and son who found level ground in the Douglas Stand to the friends who grew up together on the terraces. Belittle such experiences at your peril.

Wigan's place in my own personal and family history is clearly of great importance to me, but what justification lies within the town's claim to real historical significance? And can any evidence supporting the stance that Wigan is in some way special be found within this claim?

To be honest, I've never been a huge fan of history. It bores me. But surely no Wigan supporter can fail to be intrigued by those portentous words "Ancient And Loyal" that lie below the town's crest.

"Ancient And Loyal!"

It sounds so good, but what does it mean? How ancient? Loyal to whom?

I have, of course, diligently done my homework (if, by the word "diligently" you mean "skim-reading a few of my dad's local interest books while sat on the toilet, and checking out Wikipedia while not on the toilet").

So this is what I now know. Wigan is very, very old. It is so old that there were once lots of Romans living there or thereabouts. The reference in the town's motto to "ancient" comes from the fact that there has been a settlement at Wigan since at least AD77. And as with any ancient town, there are many fruity historical stories and legends that merge to permeate the town's character and consciousness.

Take, for instance, the story of the woman called Mabel who used to go to town without her shoes on. To be fair, she probably wasn't the first and she definitely wasn't the last. I've seen a fair few shoeless Mabels hanging around the Wigan taxi ranks late at night. It's not uncommon these days to see women heading into town in their pyjamas, even. But this particular Mabel had the distinction of being the heiress of Haigh and of being married to Sir William Bradhaigh. So you would have thought she'd have known better.

Unfortunately, her husband was implicated in a murder and, to cut a long story short, he did a runner. He returned ten years later to find that Mabel had shacked up with some Welsh bloke. This stuff is probably all extensively documented in transcripts of the Medieval version of the Jeremy Kyle show. In any case, upon his return, an enraged Sir William killed his love rival in Newton-le-Willows[3]. He then punished Mabel for her infidelity by making her walk barefoot from Haigh to Wigan every week for a year. Hence the name "Mab's Cross".

I'm not surprised. I'd be cross too if my husband behaved like that. This, though, is the folklore of Wigan. And as everybody with a modicum of superstition about them knows, folklore (be it historically accurate or not) breeds its own kind of truth. A truth that becomes part of a town and part of its people. If you've ever wondered why Wigan women are so ferocious once they get their shoes off, the answer lies with Mabel.

At some point I am going to have to mention pies, so it might as well be here. Wiganers are, after all, notorious pie eaters. It is traditionally accepted that the average Wigan resident will be besotted with pies. Mainly with meat'n'tater ones, but also with butter pies (pies made entirely out of potato and butter) and pie pies (pies made entirely out of pies).

Is this what makes Wigan special? Its pies?

It is a good question – where exactly does this "pie

---

3 Who says nothing ever happens there?

eaters" tag come from? I am particularly interested, because I have suffered from this aspersion that Wigan folk eat pies, even when I was thin. From the moment I left Wigan and arrived at my new school in Liverpool I was greeted by incessant choruses of "I like pies" (pronounced, curiously, as "aaaah laaark pies") by many of the other students and some of the teachers. At the tender age of nine I wasn't even aware of the Wigan association with pies and I mistook this gentle ribbing for genuine stupidity on their part. Once I'd deciphered their scouse attempts at a Wigan accent, I actually pitied them for their simplistic dependency on pies. These were the days before "Special Education Needs" but even then I recognised remedial behaviour when I saw it.

Later, when I discovered that they were actually just taking the mick, I felt hurt and confused. It was true, I did like pies. But I consoled myself with the thought that if the only thing they could find to criticise was my fondness for a particular type of food, then I was probably doing okay. Intrigued by their pie-themed attack on my origins, I took it upon myself to do some pie research. I had jumped to the conclusion that Wigan must have been the birth place of the pie. I had visions of moustachioed Wigan chefs of yesteryear bestowing their gift of pies upon the world.

The Invention Of The Pie – Theory One

Somewhere in the depths of Wigan, in a hall crammed with people, a door opens and the room falls silent.

The silence is broken by the squeaking of wheels as a band of chefs, haggard and weary after weeks of secretive endeavour, tentatively push the trolley that carries the fruits of their labour into the view of the waiting crowd. The shocked onlookers gasp in horror as silver domed lids are lifted to reveal platters of prototype pies.

"Oh my goodness!" members of the audience declare, "they have encased their stew in a sort of pastry housing – this is surely culinary madness!"

The hubbub eventually dies away as slices of the new food product are passed around to the delight of those present.

"It is delicious – what do you call it?" The room then falls silent once more as one of those Wigan chefs gazes upon the specimen below him and notices that the ratio of the pastry's circumference to its diameter is the same value as the ratio of a circle's area to the square of its radius.

"I call it…I call it…Pi!" he announces to the world.

"Pie?"

"Aye!"

And the rest is history. Except, of course, it isn't. Sadly that was not how the pie was born. Nor was it created by a monastic priest during a productive sojourn to the borough of Wigan. This was my second theory regarding the invention of the pie.

The Invention Of The Pie Theory Two

It is early in the eleventh century. A lone Benedictine monk, while holidaying in Wigan finds himself with a bit of time on his hands. Acting under divine guidance, and inspired by his favourite Gregorian chant ("Pie Iesu", perhaps) he is moved to create the world's first pie. Within days he is doing a roaring meat'n'tater trade from his "Ye Gregorians" market stall before having to change the name to "Ye Greggs" due to a copyright dispute with the pope.

Admittedly my second theory is riddled with flaws. For instance, there is the question of God's decision to reveal Himself to the world through the invention of the pie. What would an omniscient God, in his wisdom, feel that the birth of the pie would achieve that Jesus had not? Would the Almighty actually think that, following the miracles and supreme act of sacrifice performed by His son, what the world really needed was pie? Sadly, Ezekiel chapter 37, verse 26 does not say "Moreover I will make a covenant of pie with them." It clearly says "peas". Besides, the concept of a God who is not willing to help save his people from natural disasters, but is happy to miraculously intervene when it comes to pastry products makes little theological sense. Furthermore, why would a Benedictine monk choose Wigan for a holiday?

No, Wigan was not the birth place of the pie. Pies are so old that they predate even "Ancient" Wigan by some considerable way. History's first recorded incidents of pie production are thought to be the work of early Egyptians some two thousand years before Wigan was born. But ask yourself this – four thousand years later, who gets the credit? Do we remember Egypt as the world's pie capital? No. We associate the pie with Wigan. They get their pyramids, the Fez, and the dubious practise of gift-wrapping dead bodies, and they're welcome to all that. We, on the other hand, are remembered for the one decent thing to come out of Ancient Egypt. The pie. How many people keep the mummified remains of their relatives in their family home? How many people wear a Fez? Not many, if truth be told. How many people eat pies? I rest my case.

What about the "loyalty" bit? This must surely refer to the town's allegiance to the king during the civil war. Wigan was the scene of one of the earliest battles between royalist and parliamentary forces. It was also the location of the final battle of the war. We lost. But, considering that this loss would be the planting ground for the first seeds of democracy in England, then perhaps we shouldn't be too upset about it. Consider it the political equivalent of losing to Leeds so that Saints can't go top. Doesn't that make it feel better?

Wigan may well be ancient, and it might be loyal. It might not be the birth place of the pie, and it might be better than Egypt. All this is debatable. But one thing that you can't argue with is the town's stature in the world.

Wigan is famous, there is little question about that. Fact: everybody has heard of Wigan. Working on the basic premise of the people who audition for Britain's Got Talent, Wigan must be special. Because if it is famous, it is therefore special. And I have seen some very special people auditioning for Britain's Got Talent. They want to achieve fame through the application of the skill of singing duets with Poodles. If that's how you want to be famous, then the best of luck to you. But fame is a double edged sword, and if you're going to be famous then you are well advised to be famous for something worthy. What is Wigan famous for? Thankfully, not poodles. Not even Pooles Pies[4].

Wigan is famous for its pier. When I mention my love for the town to outsiders, the first thing I am usually asked is about the size and whereabouts of Wigan's pier. Some of them doubt it has ever existed. You could argue that they are correct, for Wigan has never really had an official pier. "Wigan Pier" is a humorous cultural reference to a jetty protruding into the canal that was used for loading barges with coal. Since the birth of this conceit, the town of Wigan has turned the joke on its head and has elevated the status of the pier to suit its own ends. Wigan pier is now very much a reality, forged from wry Lancastrian humour and immortalised in the title of the book "The Road To Wigan Pier". For the most part, those who ask me about the pier are unfamiliar with anything of George

---

4   Which don't contain poodles but do taste delicious.

Orwell's book other than the title. The very notion of a pier in Wigan has somehow entered into English cultural mythology in the same way that an absence of underpants has become part of Scotland's mythological identity. People visiting the town expect to see a pier as much as those looking up a Scotsman's kilt don't expect to see underpants.

They probably expect to see a pier (visitors to Wigan, not people looking up kilts – you'd probably be extremely surprised to see a pier up a Scotsman's kilt[5]) a bit like the ones they have seen in Blackpool and Brighton. The reality was very different. Wigan's "pier" was functional. It was and is a protuberance of man's working endeavours – a symbol of the extending aspirations of the industrious human. It is a metaphor depicting how, through hard work, impossible feats such as walking on water are achievable. You don't get that with those gaudy seaside piers, with their twinkling lights and glitzy amusements. They are all fur coat and no knickers, as my grandmother would have said. She lived in Kitt Green, so she'd have known "all fur coat and no knickers" when she saw it.

Despite this, many of the inquiries regarding Wigan's pier that I field are of a derisory nature. Even now people are still laughing at the diminutive extent of the notional Wigan pier.

The joke is on them, though. Not just because, as my wife is always telling me, size doesn't matter (she is a very

---

5   Well, perhaps not all that surprised.

short lady). But because the pier reflects all that is good and proper about Wigan. No fuss, no show. Just roll-up-the-sleeves-and-get-on-with-it practicality. The bedrock of the much talked about "Wigan Way". Furthermore, those who sneer at the pier are clearly uncultured and ignorant yobs who have never bothered to read George Orwell's books. I have even been told on several occasions, when I mention my Wigan roots, "Oh Wigan – that is where George Orwell came from."

The fools.

By that logic he was also from Paris, London and Catalonia. And he was born on a farm in 1984. Nevertheless, thanks partly to Mr Blair (Orwell's real name), Wigan is famous.

That is just one reason why Wigan is famous. There are also those people (of a certain age) who, when Wigan is mentioned, light up like fireflies and harp on about Northern Soul and keeping the faith in the Casino Club. This is another patch in Wigan's cultural tapestry, adding more than a sprinkling of flair and style to the workmanlike essence of the "Wigan Way". Not empty glitz and showmanship, it has to be said, but the sort of confident, upbeat panache that comes of having a natural talent and the strength to rise above your worries. A bit of fire in your belly that no amount of worldly woes can ever douse. This was at the core of the Northern Soul movement and is now written into the DNA of Wigan genealogy. Being born in Wigan is to be born with rhythm.

Others will extol the virtues of various different influential bands and musicians to rise from the talented hotbed of Wigan. They will talk about The Railway Children, The Verve, Starsailor and, if they really want to win my respect and admiration, the Tansads and Merry Hell[6]. Wigan is famous, you see.

St Helens is famous too. But let's not forget that St Helens (the town that has exported such riches as glass and the admittedly brilliant Jonny Vegas) is really famous only for its rugby team. We are famous anyway. Yes, it is true that if you do bring up the word "Wigan" to outsiders in conversation, most will talk only about the rugby, but there is so much more to Wigan than that.

In a Wigan-based Family Fortunes style question, though, "rugby" would definitely be your top answer. And rightly so, because if anything is ever going to encapsulate Wigan it is the cut and thrust, breathtaking flair and hard graft of what is intrinsically a family game. But Wigan is famous without the rugby, because when you look a little closer at what the town is, it becomes apparent that, when it comes down it, Wigan really is a special place. This is why it is so easy to form a lasting attachment to the town. Let people talk about the rugby, just remember that the incredible achievements and development of talent on the rugby

---

6   They won't mention Limahl, though, if they know what's good for them.

pitches of the borough might be seen by some as merely the icing on the cake of the town's flair, guile and hardiness. But they're more than that. They are our natural birthright and our destiny. They are part of our ancient folklore and the history to which we are so loyal.

It is who we are.

Mind you, I don't live in Wigan. I live in the south now, in a small and picturesque Cotswold village that lies on the Wiltshire/Gloucestershire border. It is a different world to Hindley, where I spent my infancy. It is a world of Land Rovers and chocolate Labradors. It is a world which provides an almost incessant supply of ladies on horseback trotting past your front door, all wearing wax jackets and fetching neckerchiefs. It is a world where men wear green tweed jackets and salmon-pink corduroy trousers.

Yes, we also have our problems. Gangs of Morris Dancers hanging about in pub car parks, Pimms louts on the rampage, and the elderly ladies can get a bit overheated during the village's annual flower arranging competition. To my mind, though, the biggest problem we face here is that we live in a rugby league vacuum and it prompts me to raise the second big question: why would somebody want to follow rugby league?

QUESTION TWO: IS RUGBY LEAGUE A WORTHY GAME?

I have found myself firmly embedded in rugby union territory. Here there is no expectant buzz surrounding Super League fixtures. I walk through the village on match days and the world carries on around me, oblivious to the impending clash between two tribes of rugby league's top-flight competitors. It is almost as if they don't care. This is because it is true, they actually, really, genuinely don't care. And it goes deeper than merely not caring. Living in a rugby league vacuum does not simply mean there is no appreciation of rugby league where I live. By the nature of our society it means there is also a general feeling of antipathy towards the code.

It isn't just here, in the village where I now live. I have also worked and lived in South Wales, North Yorkshire, Scotland, London, Buckinghamshire and Staffordshire. In all these places my attempts at league-flavoured conversation have, by and large, been snubbed. Not just by Union-mad rugger-buggers (many of whom actually show a healthy respect for the game), but mainly by those with little knowledge of either code. Technically these people should be equally disinterested in both sports. Yet their attitude to League is especially derogatory. They carry this perception of League as being an eccentric little oddity that never really amounts to much. They won't even watch a game because they already know they won't like it. They don't particularly like Union either, but somehow they just feel that they know that Union is something that demands respect and reverence.

I remember chatting at a cocktail party[7] to a nice lady who worked at the BBC. In particular I remember her staring at me incredulously and saying, with unguarded astonishment, "Oh, so you actually like shiny-shorts rugby!"

Nor will I forget the sneering, contemptuous remarks of a Bath supporter during the cross code challenge game at Twickenham as she first deigned to notice the Wigan fans. "My goodness," she said with the sort of contempt you could actually taste, "they're just like soccer fans!"

"My goodness," I replied, "you're just like a mindless, insular, bigot." I think she got the message.

Other attempts to raise the topic of my passion for the sport have generally met with derision and disapproval. The most common response from Union aficionados is usually along the lines of "But how could you possibly enjoy such a boring game, it is just so stop-start-stop-start! How boring is that?"

Indeed.

How boring is that? When compared to their game which, in my mind, is more a case of "Stop…"

---

7   Not in Wigan, obviously. You don't get cocktail parties in Wigan. You don't even get cocktails in Wigan. The most adventurous thing you're likely to see somebody do to a drink in Wigan is to pour some brown ale into their mild – crazy!

They tell me I am mistaken and that there are hidden subtleties to behold during such Union intricacies as rucks, mauls and scrummages. There may well be many subtle intricacies involved in several grown men squirming around on top of each other for ten minutes. But they're not necessarily the sort of intricacies that I want to find out about.

This is the default setting of rugby union. A pile of men. They even score tries like that. They'll form a scrum which will then "flollup" in the general direction of the try line. Then, once his passion for flolluping has been satisfied, the referee will tell the world that a try has been scored (he's got to be guessing, hasn't he?).

Personally, I like to know there's still a ball on the pitch. But let's not be too hasty or dismissive of the Union code. Not all of the game is spent hiding the ball under piles of writhing men. A lot of it is spent kicking the ball out of play. This generally initiates something known as a "line-out" which is when the tallest men on the pitch get to satisfy their secret yearnings to be ballet dancers. Be fair, how else are men of that build going to get to do something vaguely like Nureyev without being laughed at? The most successful ballerinas (or at least the ones on the same team as the bloke throwing the ball in) then get to pass the ball back to one of their team mates. Depending on his own personal preference, he will then either kick it off the pitch again or roll around on the floor with it, beckoning a mob of squirming men to lie on top of him.

Of course, there are many, many instances in rugby union of free-flowing, fast running, ball-playing rugby. These are the times when it is indistinguishable from rugby league.

I might sound as one-sided and as biased as the rugby union enthusiasts who belittle my favourite game, but at least I can claim to have attempted to play rugby union. Once. It was while I was at university in South Wales and the English students were invited to take on the College's First XV. What ensued was an aching, grinding encounter knee deep in mud. The entire game seemed to be spent in piles of writhing bodies. And there was a lot of stamping. After fifty minutes we had irreparably damaged all of our substitutes, we had then borrowed one from the Welsh team and had finally ended up desperately begging the sole surviving spectator to don a pair of boots and help us out. She wasn't interested though.

While I am prepared to accept that people might take some sort of perverse satisfaction from playing the game, rugby union has no real claim to be a spectator sport. Rugby league, on the other hand, is designed for the spectator and every innovation made in the game that is not for the safety of the players is made for the benefit of the spectator. There is no question about this. Rugby league had to adapt and evolve in order to bring in the paying customers. Following the Northern Union's split from the RFU – a split necessitated by the need to retain and support working class players – the game had to keep people coming in through the turnstiles just to survive.

And lying at the core of this clash of the codes is an uncomfortable truth about culture and class in England. Rugby union has always had the support of the upper classes. Rugby league might at one point have been able to flash the cash to entice rugby union's stars, but money in itself has never been enough. Union has always had establishment, money, marketing, the Old Boys' Network and the trappings of privilege. In comparison rugby league has always been something of a Robin Hood. "Shiny Shorts Rugby" has never been an honest description of what rugby league is, nor has "Stop-Start-Stop-Start Rugby". These are just the straw-grasping criticisms that arise from a culture of Haves versus Have Nots. Those who Have will say almost anything to justify and retain their position, regardless of the real truth (or lack of it) behind the words. I don't mind people preferring rugby union to rugby league. I just want to hear some real, genuine reasons for it and some honesty. Is that too much to ask?

Being a rugby league supporter sometimes feels like you are walking around with a chip on your shoulder, and that is how many people will describe your overly defensive stance and your healthy distrust of the other code. They're wrong, though. It is a matter of principle. It is born out of honesty and true working class values. The Union aficionados will talk about principles and about how real gentlemen required no financial incentive to play their gentlemen's game. What does that really mean, though? It means that they favoured a code of class segregation. They were looking down their noses at people they would rather not be rubbing shoulders with. In the attitudes that people, even today, have towards rugby league I detect that there's a fair bit of that old snobbery still around.

Regardless of the merits and demerits of either code (because they both have their faults and flaws as spectator sports) there is a simple and straightforward line drawn between them. On one side lies a game of honesty and integrity that has always welcomed everybody. On the other side lies a game that has a core of arrogance, prejudice and xenophobic selfishness. I know which side of that line I stand on. Me? I'm rugby league, through and through.

I have dwelt on the other code for long enough. There are other sports out there, after all.

A few years ago I was having my hair cut in a barber's shop in the West London town of Acton. Having exhausted the usual chit chat that forms the mainstay of the relationship between the snipper and the snippee – "What about this weather, then?", "Going anywhere nice this year?" and "Touch my daughter again and I'll chop your ears off, sunshine," – we got onto the subject of sport. I told him of my love for rugby league and he snorted and shook his head. I was expecting the usual rah-rah spiel to come gushing out over my half-trimmed head, and had prepared myself accordingly. But it turned out that my barber had a problem not just with rugby league but with team games in general.

"No," he said, "these team sports show no true measure of the individual athlete. In a team game an individual can hide behind other players." He sighed deeply. "Its just not the same," he added before sending me to sleep with a rehearsed speech about the many joys of athletics, with references to physiological and anatomical detail that you would have associated more with a butcher than a barber. I stopped going there after that. Not just because I was worried he might turn me into pies, but mainly because he clearly hadn't seen a game of rugby league in his life. Hiding behind other players indeed!

Oh, Mr Hairdresser, there are no passengers in rugby league.

Besides, the individual athlete might well be able to show off his or her prowess, skill and strength without the perceived help of others, but, as much as I admire individual skills, the thing I love to see most is teamwork.

I like to watch men with a common mission working together, making the most of their individual skills but ultimately being prepared to do whatever is necessary for the good of the team. There lies the magic. To quote the Wonderpets – "What kind of work? Teamwork!"

The camaraderie and the self-sacrifice. "All for one and one for all!" (to quote the Muskahounds, for those who are too old to have seen the Wonderpets[8]).

That's what does it for me. That's why I find it hard to

---

8   And "flobbadobbadobba" for those who are to old to remember the Muskahounds.

identify a favourite player. I love the team too much. And there have been so many wonderful individuals parading their skills in the cherry and white jersey, many of them playing in the same team together. How do you choose between Shaun Edwards and Andy Farrell? Or Ellery Hanley and Andy Gregory? Or Sam Tomkins and Pat Richards? Yes, you can start weighing in with various Top Trumps-esque stuff like "Wiganess", but it is all so vague, forced and subjective. My first ever favourite player was Martin Foy and that was just because I liked his hair style.

My Acton barber would probably have approved of that.

Born of the working classes and tempered by honour and values. A team game, where everybody works together. You get what you see. No frills, but more than a little flair. Much like Wigan itself.

Honest hard graft and bit of style. These aren't just rugby qualities, they are life skills. And they're as good a starting point as any for someone stepping out into the world. And it will do me, because no matter what the future holds, or how long it takes, I am Wigan till I die. That is who I am, it is who we are as Wigan supporters.

Descartes had his "I think therefore I am". Wiganosophers have "I am Wigan till I die."

TRADITIONS:
STICK, TWIST OR BUST?

You simply cannot beat a decent bit of tradition. It is, after all, a very important part of our social identity. Tradition is the platform that we build our lives and deeds around, and the thing we turn to when we find ourselves faced with the unfamiliar. It informs our judgements and infuses our day to day existence with meaning and purpose. Tradition is like a lovely, big, comfy, security blanket. We adore tradition, and we shout of our love for it from the rooftops. Quite simply, tradition is great stuff. But this is only true assuming that you are talking about the right bits of tradition, as opposed to the wrong bits of tradition. They can be quite ghastly, those wrong bits and most people would agree that the wrong bits are best avoided.

You would hope that it would be easy to single out the positive traditions. Instinct would have you believe that the positive traditions would be the good, old fashioned, traditional things that you know you can always rely on. Things like the law.

But just how clear is the law? And how reliable? Take murder, for instance. As everybody will be quick to tell you (if you threaten them enough), murder is illegal. But it would be a mistake to think that it is always illegal. For instance, according to my research[9], you are well within your rights to kill a Scottish man who is carrying a bow and arrow through the streets of York. It's fine then, obviously.

On the other hand, while a spot of Scot-slaughtering is apparently all well and good in York, throughout the rest of Britain it is illegal to eat mince pies on Christmas Day. Apparently they encourage gluttony. Personally, I think it would be better to ban sprouts. They don't encourage gluttony, but they do make pulling crackers in the vicinity of Aunty Margaret a potential fire risk. Judging by the sounds and smells that emanate from her chair during Christmas dinner, sprouts don't agree with her. If she ever ignites after eating a portion of sprouts she'll be harder to put out than an erupting volcano. It will be like Mount Vesuvius all over again.

The law also states that a man with a moustache may never kiss a woman in public, which is fair enough. Nobody wants to see that. Similarly, it is illegal for a woman to be topless in Liverpool, unless she works in a tropical fish shop. I spent much of my youth visiting Liverpool's tropical fish shops, hoping to admire the wild guppies on display. Sadly, all I ever saw was tropical fish.

---

9   I use the word "research" in its loosest possible form here. This is stuff I "Googled" and I haven't the slightest clue about the veracity of the claims made. But they do sound good.

There are some strange foreign laws too. In Switzerland, a man may not urinate while standing up after 10pm. It's just too darned dangerous. In Ohio it is illegal to get a fish drunk. And if you own a bar in Ohio, you are breaking the law if you allow a customer to pretend to have sex with an imaginary buffalo on the dance floor. I'm not exactly sure what that would look like, but I expect it would involve direct contravention of the daylight rule between the customer and the imaginary buffalo.

These are mad, stupid, ridiculous laws. But they've got one thing in common. They're ancient. And they've been kept in place out of a sense of tradition. People won't budge away from them because…well, because we've always had them. This is the curse of tradition. Traditions are arbitrary and don't always fit the time and the place. I am put in mind of fathers on holiday, dragging their kids to the beach, fondly flicking through their own memories of sunny Tuesday mornings on happy holiday beaches.

"We always go to the beach on Tuesday mornings when we're on holiday," they proclaim. While the rain is bouncing off their heads. And the whole family is being sandblasted to shreds in the gale force 12 winds. As tsunamis bull-doze the beach huts.

Even faced with scenes of such devastation, your average tradition-crazed father will still be battling to erect his deckchair with a forced smile while pointing out that, looking on the bright side, he's managed to claim the best spot on the beach.

31

People cling on to ridiculous, outdated, obsolete notions just because they are traditions. There's a word for this – "fundamentalism" and it is prevalent in every walk of life from religion to rugby league.

Of course, not all traditions are bad, just as not all traditions are good. The problem we face, as Wiganosphers, is in trying to separate the good ones from the bad ones. To expose the dodgy and to uphold the positive. The other problem we face is that we all think the ones we like are the positive ones.

I know what rugby league traditions I like. I know what feels good and proper and traditional about rugby matches to me. The smells, the sights and the noises – those blood-curdling howls to be heard at rugby grounds up and down the country.

"Forrr-ward!"

"Gerrrrum-onside!"

You know where you are when you hear those calls. You are at a rugby league ground, enjoying the tradition of bizarre shouting. Then there is "Reff-errr-eeeeeh!" which I have always thought sounds a little too camp to be associated with rugby league; and yet there it is, happily and effeminately mincing away, oblivious to the rest of the macho shouts around it.

There is also, of course, the famous cherry-and-white battle cry that is now so familiar I believe it happens almost without thought. It just occurs all by itself whenever Wigan supporters gather in a number exceeding ten (or three, if they've been drinking). It is like an automated answering system, or some hypnosis-induced chant. No effort or preparation is required, it just happens in much the same naturalistic way that breathing occurs. It goes like this: "Wiiii-gan! Wiiii-gan! Wiii-gan! Wiii-gan!" Et cetera.

I will not forget how as a child attending one of my first matches I was startled when a flat capped gentleman behind me tapped me on the shoulder and asked me why I wasn't joining in with this chant. I told him (rather cleverly, I thought) that it was because I didn't know the words. I later surmised that, despite his appearance, he must have been a chief advertising executive because a couple of years later I saw the very same dialogue being used in a Skoll lager advert.

Group chanting is a tradition that fascinates me, but even more intriguing are the sporadic cries which will occasionally interrupt the fervour of group chanting. I do love the sudden, spontaneous remarks, outbursts or questions aimed at players, match officials or whichever deity happens to be in attendance.

One season I had the genuine pleasure to be sat behind an old man who, upon seeing an outside back catch the ball, would persist in shouting "OPEN...YOUR... LEGS!" – words I would previously have expected to be reserved solely for brothels and maternity wards.

My personal favourite spontaneous call from the terraces is an emphatic demand I heard only a couple of years back – "Come on Wigan, stop playing with your food!"

It had a certain charm and subtlety of humour that I felt was lacking in the "F★★★ing f★★k Wigan, for f★★k's sake f★★★ing sort your f★★★ing selves out [*brief pause – possibly for effect*]…F★★k!" which had immediately preceded it.

It wasn't the sort of outburst we were used to in the West Stand, and it was closely followed by two cardiac arrests and the sad, ironic sound of an elderly gentleman choking to death on an Uncle Joe's Mintball. Sometimes they don't keep you all aglow. Sometimes they make you go alternately purple and white.

But this was an understandable reaction to such language among many of my fellow West-Standers, for these are people who were brought up in an era of gentility. They are the supporters of yesteryear, who in many cases are sacrificing sizeable chunks of an insult of a pension just to cling onto one of the few constants in their lives – the Cherry And Whites. They've seen so much change. The ground that once felt firm beneath their feet is now a sea of drifting sand. Yet the Cherry And Whites stand firm, ancient and loyal. Wigan RL – their touchstone, their link to a past they felt comfortable with. These people are Cherry And White to the core, and they don't like it when the air turns blue.

The TV special "Warriors Down Under" which documented the club's 2014 sojourn to Sydney for the World Club Challenge left many of my West Stand compatriots aghast. The language used by Wigan's head coach was, in the eyes (and ears) of many, both unprofessional and unnecessary. As somebody who is in no way averse to a bit of fruity language, I have to admit that even I found it disappointing.

Now, I am probably one of Shaun Wane's biggest fans. I have a huge amount of admiration and respect for him and for what he has achieved. Moreover, I know that dressing room discussions aren't going to sound like a scene from Biggles. I am perfectly comfortable in the understanding that the language used in such circumstances isn't going to be worthy of your maiden aunt. I just don't think it was a good move to broadcast it.

A bit of sensitive editing could have achieved two goals. It could have made Shaun Wane sound almost Churchillian and it could have spared a good section of the audience offense.

In the event neither of these things happened. I know spectators who even today still feel aggrieved by that broadcast. Furthermore, the coverage didn't make Shaun Wane sound Churchillian. If anything it made him sound rather limited. Somehow I very much doubt that this is a fair representation of the man.

A bit more attention to the details of our sport's long-standing traditions and values would have seen the whole thing handled differently.

Some might say that this is one area where the game and the audience should move with the times and that people should just accept the sort of language that is in general usage. I do have some sympathy for this view. There are all kinds of areas where the boundaries of acceptable language can and should be pushed. In literature, for instance, and in stand-up comedy. But not in rugby league. I just don't see what it can achieve.

I always cringe when a player "accidentally" swears during the post-match interview. The language doesn't offend me, but I know it will offend others and my real sympathies lie with those people. In particular they lie with the older spectators. I feel for them, and I get particularly irked by the derision of West Stand clientele by younger supporters who refer to it as "The Grave Yard." It is one thing to gravitate to the stand that suits you best, but quite another to openly mock and deride your fellow supporters. Besides, I've been party to some of the most highly charged celebrations imaginable in "The Grave Yard". Those wrinklies can freak out with the best of them at the sight of a length of the pitch try. And in the West Stand you have the added entertainment of watching the St John Ambulance volunteers twitching nervously whenever the pensioners start waving their arms in the air. Like they don't know which one to rush to first. Furthermore, in which other stand will you hear, repeatedly throughout the match, those immortal words... "OPEN...YOUR...LEGS!"

These things make me very happy.

That is how I decide which traditions are the good traditions. They are the ones that make me happy. Even sad traditions like the minute's silence to commemorate the loss of members of our community make me happy. Such traditions might not seem outwardly cheerful, but there is still a warmth and appreciation to be gleaned from them. Standing together shoulder to shoulder, in silence, showing our respect and appreciation. It is more than just a paying of respects. It is an act of defiance. Death might claim the lives of the people we love, but our defiant silence makes one thing very clear. Death doesn't win. Because at that very moment thousands of people are gathered together remembering the gift of a single life. While we are prepared to make this statement, we demonstrate our commitment to ensure that those we have lost will remain in our hearts forever. Suddenly death seems impotent and toothless. That makes me happy.

Singing "Abide With Me" is another tradition that can be described as outwardly morose. Taken at face value, it is a slow, soulful song pleading for god's support at the moment of death. Before my first visit to Wembley I dismissed that hymn as a morbid dirge. And I stood by that judgement right up until the point when I rose to my feet in order to sing it (badly) in unison with thousands of my fellow rugby league supporters. Since then it has never failed to make the hairs on the back of my neck stand on end. Context is everything. The sense of occasion and the raw camaraderie of the experience made me re-assess my opinion. I read and re-read the lyrics to myself on the train home after my first ever Wembley final.

Abide with me; fast falls the eventide;
The darkness deepens; Lord with me abide.
When other helpers fail and comforts flee,
Help of the helpless, O abide with me.

There is no denying the fact that those lyrics bring to mind the hardest of times. Yet the act of singing the hymn together as members of the rugby league fellowship, rather than as supporters of a team, is immensely uplifting. It transcends team colours and parochial allegiances. This is something bigger and grander. Abide With Me reminds us that we are really all together in the same struggle, and from that we gain strength. Moreover, it sums up the true spirit of rugby league. The battle and the camaraderie. We will take on the world, we will do it together and we will be there for each other, come what may. Is that not exactly what it means to be a rugby league supporter? Abide With Me has been sung at every Challenge Cup Final for almost one hundred years. Long may it continue. It makes me happy.

At the time of writing, I am not especially happy, though. This is because I am in mourning for my pants. I am currently having to deal with the sad loss of my favourite "lucky" underpants. These were the pants I used to compulsively wear to every rugby game I attended. Please understand that this is something I find very difficult to talk about. They were lovely once, those beloved, colourful stripy hipsters of mine – I bought them from "Gap". Admittedly, they are a good deal less colourful now, but the stripes are still vaguely noticeable in a faded, greying sort of way. Seven years of non-stop use will do that to your undies. But these undies went before their time. They were the victim of a tragic incident.

My wife found them.

We were visiting my parents' home in Ashton-In-Makerfield, staying with them over the weekend of a crucial Wigan Warriors home fixture. Upon our arrival, Mrs Macaulay took it upon herself to unpack my bag. I was still boiling the kettle as she told me that she was going upstairs to unpack and, distracted as I was, I simply grunted in agreement. It had been a long drive and I was tired. I had forgotten all about the contents of my bag – the secret I had been hiding from her for all these years.

Minutes later I heard the horrified cry from our bedroom. I knew at once what had happened. She had found my lucky pants.

I raced up the stairs, taking them three at a time, and burst into the room. Sure enough, there she was, holding aloft my lucky undies in a manner akin to the way the late Steve Irwin would hold up a highly venomous snake. With real caution.

And she shot me a look – a horrible look – as if to say that she felt she didn't know who I was anymore.

"What are these?" she demanded.

"My underpants," I mumbled in response.

"Look at them!"

"I know." They looked like they had been subjected to a prolonged nuclear and chemical attack. It was hard to know what to say. My wife knew what to say though.

"Where's the bloody gusset?"

I gazed at the frayed, worn edges of the gaping hole that had once been the location of the business end of my underpants. And I shrugged like a guilty schoolboy.

"How long have you had these?" She asked, waving them in my face. I wanted to tell her to be gentle with them, that they were fragile, but I guessed that this would only emphasise her point. Instead I tried to appeal to her more reasonable nature. I told her that they were my lucky pants. A terrible misunderstanding ensued. Fortunately, I just about managed to talk her round and, although she didn't quite understand my tradition of lucky underpants, she did eventually agree that it was the sad, pathetic sort of measure that I would sink to.

"You, don't get it!" I protested, "it's what you do when you're a fan. It's doing your bit. It's part of the support!"

"Well," she said, "you can't be getting much support from these," and with that she whisked them off to the bin.

My lucky pants are gone forever. The sense of loss I feel is compounded with a very real feeling of dread and terror. How can Wigan be expected to win any match if I am not wearing my lucky pants for the duration of the game? This is the crux (and crotch) of the matter. I have become convinced that my underwear has some sort of bearing on the outcome of professional rugby league games.

I know how it sounds. It sounds like I am completely mad. I don't need to be told this, I am a rational human being. I do not feel compelled to worship or pray to any kind of deity. I cannot accept the existence of ghosts. I fully embrace scientific principles regarding the creation and nature of the universe, and I have no truck with concepts such as fate or destiny. And yet I have mentally endowed my underpants with the magical power to change the outcome of events that, empirically speaking, do not concern them. To make matters worse, I engage in ritualistic behaviour prior to putting them on. Not only is it important that I wear the pants, but it is equally important that I correctly perform the appropriate rites in order to unleash the true potency of their magic. I don't want to say too much about this ritual, but it does involve the use of copious amounts of aftershave and some gentle rubbing (which probably explains the disappearance of the gusset).[10] All this, of course, achieves nothing. How could it do otherwise? There is no conceivable way in which my underpants could influence the outcome of a rugby match (unless, of course, I was to attempt streaking). There isn't a single player in the team who gives a thought to my pants prior to taking to the pitch (I hope) and no member of the coaching staff has ever contacted me to ask about the mystical qualities of my underwear. Despite this, I have always insisted on wearing them. In fact I have never been able to bring myself to not wear them at a rugby game. I can't explain it. It is a wild pocket of superstition in my otherwise rational and balanced outlook. It is not even as if my wearing the pants has always resulted in a win to

---

10 At this point I wish to make it clear that there is nothing remotely sexual about this procedure and that it is carried out under controlled conditions in a private and secure environment – usually the book cupboard at the back of my classroom.

Wigan. There have been many times when I have been in my lucky pants and Wigan have lost. I suspect that this is the subconscious reason behind my invention of the pre-pants ritual. So as not to shake my faith in the pants, I have created an opportunity for human error to impede their ability. "Oh," I say to myself following a loss, "it must be because I didn't quite rub the club badge properly against the pants after I applied the aftershave."

I do hope I am not mad. In fact, upon consideration of this rather bizarre behaviour, I recently took steps to find out whether I was alone in having a strange pre-match tradition. Or lucky pants. I felt that if I could ascertain the existence of a number of other individuals with similar traditions, then it would be a strong indication that I wasn't mad and that such behaviour is a normal part of being a rugby league supporter. With some trepidation, I ventured onto the internet message boards. I'd heard about some of the people who hang out in there – stories of weird and colourful characters who lurk there waiting to ensnare passers-by in meaningless and slightly threatening conversations. Quite frankly it sounded like an online version of The Moon Under Water. So it was a little nervously that I broke my "thread virginity" (which is not at painful as it sounds) and I keyed in the following question:

"What sort of curious and bizarre pre-match rituals and traditions do you cling onto?"

Then I waited. I didn't have to wait long, though. This was, after all, the world-wide-web – the encyclopaedia that never sleeps. A never-ending, fathomless ocean of knowledge and facts. A mine of information that never runs dry. If I was going to find answers to my question somewhere, then I would definitely find them here.

Sure enough, within minutes an answer came my way. And this was it:-

> *"I quite often buy a Cadbury's Double-Decker."*

I still felt mad.

Nonetheless, I will continue to observe my tradition of lucky pants. While the old ones have now been dispatched to the local land-fill site, I bought a new pair soon afterwards that now sit in readiness for the forthcoming season. I have even done the ritual. And I did it in the bathroom by candlelight, for added potency. In the flickering orange glow, I stood on the threshold where tradition meets superstition between the towel rail and the toilet. It seems incongruous that a devotee of the "13" man code should be overly worried about superstition. Anybody who is of a superstitious disposition would probably avoid the sport like the plague. Yet to fans of the game, the number thirteen has become a favourite number. It has taken on a life of its own. It is embraced and loved. It is even a rallying cry. I was once asked, upon moving into a new house, if I was worried about living in a house that bore the number 13 on the door. Of course I wasn't – to my way of thinking, this was just another of the house's many selling points. The number felt right to me. Rugby league has eradicated any previous superstitions that I might have harboured. But it has supplanted them with superstitions of its own. Swimming as they do against the flow of my rational and pragmatic outlook on life, they manifest themselves in bizarre pre-match rituals that have now become traditions in their own right. Gusset or not, my lucky pants are a relatively harmless, if peculiar, match-day tradition.

Another match-day tradition that may well be peculiar to me is that of being with my dad and watching as he lets on to somebody he doesn't actually know. It happens a lot. This is not to say that he is one of those gibbering madmen you find hanging around outside Bargain Booze outlets. He's not like them, he just shares a common pastime with them – accosting strangers and engaging them in conversation as if he has known them for years. It is, in fact, quite understandable in my dad's case because he does know practically everybody. Being a vicar who has at some point broken the bread and spilled the wine in most (if not all) of Wigan's Anglican churches, he does have a wide circle of friends. This circle widened considerably upon his retirement, since which time he has become a "collar for hire" specialising in weddings and funerals. The chances are he has married or buried someone you know. If not, he has probably baptised someone you know. For instance, he actually baptised former referee Karl Kirkpatrick many years ago. And following some of the games that Mr Kirkpatrick presided over, he would have been only too happy to do his funeral too.

My sister and I have always had to get used to stopping every twenty yards or so en route to various rugby grounds in order for him to exchange niceties with various acquaintances of his – something that is actually very pleasant and affirming. But it is also side-splittingly funny when he stops somebody (whom he clearly doesn't know) dead in his or her tracks to ask how they are getting on. I just love their bewildered expressions and ad hoc responses. Most people are nice enough to play along and some will even engage for several minutes in a conversation about things they know nothing about. Once a wide-eyed, bald man did become extremely agitated and threaten physical violence (never a good idea with my dad because he'll be only too quick to take you up on the offer) but most of the conversations are perfectly pleasant. On one occasion he even exchanged phone numbers with a complete stranger. We never ask about what went on there.

We do tend to ask, as we move away from the bewildered victim, "did you actually even know him?" To which, the response is usually "I'm not sure but its better to be safe than sorry."

So, if you've ever been accosted by an unknown, eager vicar at a rugby match while his offspring stand to one side not trying hard enough to contain their amusement, let me apologise now on his behalf. He thought he recognised you and didn't like to take the chance.

Of course, the real problem with this habit of my father's is that the people he tends to make a bee-line for are often those players, coaches or minor celebrities who he has seen on the telly but can't quite place. We have witnessed some really riveting exchanges with the Bill Arthurs and Dave Hadfields of this world. And there was a period in the late eighties and early nineties when Colin Welland must have been concerned that he had a stalker. And a religious one at that.

I suppose I should show a little more sympathy for Mr Welland, because I too have suffered the humiliation of being mistaken for somebody completely different at a rugby match. It was in the bar after a game when, as I was ordering a pint, I was approached by Harrison Hansen's father who proceeded to start a strange conversation with me. I gaped back at him, wide-eyed and open-mouthed, as I tried to figure out how best to respond. Seeing his mistake, he apologised profusely and explained that he had mistaken me for Max – the Wigan mascot. At this point I nearly choked on my beer. How exactly is that supposed to make it better? I'm still not entirely sure how or why I resemble Max, but every time that character runs out onto the pitch looking, as he does, like a clueless, grinning moron with those mackerel flapping about on top of his hat, I feel a pang of despair. That's what I look like, apparently. I don't wish to sound at all antagonistic towards our beloved Max (he is, after all, a ruthless warrior) and I appreciate his value in adding an extra dimension to younger supporters. I'm just not his greatest fan, that's all.

I don't remember there being any such mascots parading before my eyes at Central Park when I was a little boy. Now, this might just be because I'm getting on a bit and my memory is playing tricks on me. Or perhaps I have subconsciously edited such things out of my childhood memories. It could even be that when you are little you just don't notice the mascots. It may well be the case that your youthful willingness to accept the presence of large cartoon characters with frozen expressions as a normal part of life means that you just don't register them. In which case you'd have to wonder what the point of them is, because they're not the easiest of illusions to pull off, even when they're done well. I speak with the benefit of experience. I had the misfortune to be employed for a brief period of time as a furry mascot on a family holiday park. I was Bradley Bear.

Bradley Bear certainly occupied the upper echelons of the hierarchy of mascots. I quickly learned that the Bradley Bear costume was afforded the sort of awed respect that you would normally associate with senior members of the Roman Catholic Church and the Crown Jewels. On that camp site, being in the presence of Bradley Bear was the next best thing to an audience with his holiness the Pope. You didn't mess with the bear. The costume included a humungous, startled-looking bear head complete with an interior cooling system that was basically a small fan, a bit of wire and three AA batteries. This elaborate set-up was referred to as "the hardware" and was treated like it was the cutting edge of scientific endeavour. I lost count of the number of times I was told not to interfere with the hardware – it was precious! As was almost every aspect of Bradley Bear. Nothing about that bear was taken for granted. Together with all the other new recruits, I was forced to sit through a two-hour lecture on Bradley Bear Protocol.

- *Bradley Bear never wears anything other than the official costume.*
- *Bradley Bear never accepts or eats sweets.*
- *Bradley Bear never uses play-violence.*
- *Bradley Bear does not speak.*
- *Bradley Bear never drinks or smokes.*
- *Bradley Bear never appears semi-dressed or without his head on.*
- *Bradley Bear does not have a birthday.*

Half way through this torrent of Bradley Bear etiquette, I put up my hand and asked the obvious question.

"Does Bradley Bear shit in the woods?"

My days of being Bradley Bear were sadly limited. After my "refusal to appreciate the gravitas of the company mascot" I ended up being shuffled over to DJ duties after the bingo.

That company certainly took their mascot seriously and, in all fairness, it paid off. Bradley Bear was a successful mascot. This was presumably as a result of the effort that went into maintaining his image.

Compare this to my earliest memory of a mascot on the pitch at Wigan. It was a mangy, flea-bitten black cat in cheap trainers. Prior to the game, it would roam the perimeter of the pitch (quite possibly marking its territory as it did so) and it would occasionally fling its arms and legs about in wild spasms. It did this as if to say "despite appearances to the contrary, I am actually still alive."

Eventually this cat was replaced (I am presuming it was put down) by a giant pie. The pie didn't last long either[11]. In order to be successful, there are a number of things that a mascot needs to be able to do. It needs to have character and a certain amount of charm. It also needs a degree of mobility in order to take part in those "hilarious" mascot races. A pie, though, is just a pie. There's not much character there, really. Only filling. As for mobility, its size and shape ensured that it would encounter severe wind resistance even when it was standing still. It appeared for a handful of games (on days when the wind was low) before vanishing altogether. Then, at the time that the club adopted the "warriors" label, we were treated to a group of new mascots. Unlike the cat and the pie, these new arrivals were not hiding beneath furry masks or comedy rubber suits. They were a group of well-proportioned male and female models, with long, flowing locks and full-on scanty warrior gear. They even had real swords, which would have made the mascot races interesting. To say that they seemed out of place on

---

11 Pies don't tend to last long in Wigan. Walking around Central Park disguised as a massive pie is an incredibly dangerous undertaking, and not something I would advise anybody to do.

the pitch of a family-oriented rugby match would be an understatement. They looked like they'd been kidnapped from a bisexual Scandinavian lap dancing club. Thousands of us looked on, mesmerised by them, as they romped around the pitch in a well-crafted display of high-camp expressionism with lashings of faux machismo. "What next?" I remember thinking.

The answer was Winston The Warrior. In many ways it was something of a relief to see a return to a genuine over-sized rubber caricature. Sadly, there was something not quite right about Winston. For whatever reason – and these things can be particularly difficult to pin down – he just didn't gel. In my opinion he looked too much like Dawn French. With Fluella Benjamin's hair and Xena The Warrior Princess's costume. As far as warriors go, you had to wonder just exactly how effective he would be in battle. It wasn't long before he too vanished, to be replaced (for reasons I cannot even begin to fathom) by a gorilla. Kelvin at least won the admiration of the fans in a way that no other mascot had been able to. Let's face it, everybody loves a cheeky monkey.

And now we have Max who, apparently, looks like me. Like many rugby league supporters, I feel he sits somewhat awkwardly within our hallowed arena. Mascots are not particularly traditional, and that is part of the problem. Rugby league is a game that is steeped in tradition. It is almost a tradition in itself. For years and years rugby league branded and marketed itself as a game of time-honoured customs and values. It looked out at a changing world from under its flat cap and said, "Never mind your namby-pamby, fancy, lah-de-dah new doings, here in rugby league land we stick to what we know". It garnered respect and admiration for this no-nonsense, bloody-minded attitude. Good old fashioned muck and blood, with a plethora of glorious tries thrown in for good measure. But you cannot ignore the march of progress forever, and there were occasions when the game was in danger of becoming a caricature in itself. Farcical moments, such as the Eddie Waring "dog-on-a-pitch" incident, threatened to expose the sport as an increasingly anachronistic spectacle. Ironically, Eddie Waring was initially criticised within rugby league's enclaves for being far too concerned with new-fangled follies in his attempts to widen the game's appeal. Later he was lampooned and pilloried for his archaic and overtly northern delivery which many claimed was holding the game back. Dichotomy has always been a traditional aspect of rugby league.

Sooner or later the game was going to have to accept significant change, and it certainly did so following its 1995 centenary season. The next year saw change and upheaval on a scale unparalleled in any other domestic sport. As supporters, we witnessed a wholesale cull of some of the traditional aspects of rugby league that we once considered to be sacrosanct. For many people the ushering in of the super league era was a distinctly painful process. The gallant leap into the summer and the re-structuring of the league was too much for many dyed in the wool traditionalists. And for a middle class, public school educated, liberal minded reader of The Guardian like myself, there were even greater challenges ahead.

The advent of Super League turned me into a Sun reader. It was a difficult transition to face, but in some ways I was helped by my immediate environment. At the time, I was working in a department store in London called Bentalls of Ealing and passing through the tradesman's entrance with a rolled copy of the Sun under your arm was considered de rigueur for all employees. The reason I took to reading the Sun was because of the weekly Super League supplement in the back. I also quite liked the semi-naked ladies nearer the front. Aside from this regular special feature in the Sun, I was suffering from the effects of a relative dearth of rugby league news. It was London, after all. But lo and behold – tucked away in the Sun of all places, was a weekly section devoted to my favourite game. There it was – available nation-wide and vaunting the excitement and importance of the sport. This was one of the developments that sold the notion of the Super League to me.

Looking back, those seemed like exciting days. New names, colourful new strips and badges, and a seemingly bright future for rugby league. Backed by the wealth and power of News Ltd, the empire behind Sky TV and newspapers like the Sun, it felt like there would be no stopping the sport. Rugby league was going global. The wave of optimism was always tempered by an amount of trepidation and heartache. The ensuing transformation might have been welcome, but it was very clear that it was coming at a price. Traditional branding and clubs had no place in the new Super League universe. Not even longstanding comforts like identity were immune from the tampering. It was at this point that we changed our name. Overnight we became someone else. No longer were we the good, old fashioned and trustworthy Wigan Rugby League Football Club. Suddenly we were Warriors.

I wasn't the only one who questioned this move into what I considered to be the territory of imported fast food franchises. I remember how, back in 1992, I had a stand up row with an employee at a Wimpey restaurant regarding the company's decision to rebrand what had traditionally been referred to as a "sausage sandwich" and choosing instead the term "bender in a bun." It infuriated me.

"It won't sell," I told him, in what was admittedly the slurred verbage of somebody who had been drinking all day and was therefore resorting to Wimpey food due to a lack of higher reasoning. He pointed out that I was already disproving my own argument, as he served me my hot bender. My real point, though, was not that the new name would put people off, but that it made no difference. It was redundant. If I wanted a sausage sandwich and ended up with a bender, I'd still be happy to exactly the same degree. The bender in a bun was marketing for marketing's sake. It was the same with the adoption of the "Warriors" tag.

Many voices were raised against it for all kinds of reasons. Some people rallied against it because it flew in the face of tradition. It was rugby league heresy. Tradition is all well and good, of course, and I like it. But, by and large, heresy is far more entertaining, so I couldn't add my voice to those of the objectors on those grounds.

I did read an article somewhere that claimed the changing of the club's name to Wigan Warriors would work to the team's detriment because the players would subconsciously register the new name and, as if by magic, turn into actual real warriors. They would become battle-hardened soldiers, losing any creativity, flair and finesse that they might have had. Instead they would strive to win games through the tactics of attritional warfare, wearing down their opponents with relentless waves of dreary attack. The name change alone, the writer insisted, would turn Wigan into a team of mindless, grinding forwards. The writer cited the Auckland Warriors as an example of how this had already happened at another club.

I must admit that at first I was impressed by this argument. The pseudo-biblical concept of the power that names have over the owners – the notion that somehow we become the name – seemed a good one. However, six months after changing my own name to "Matt Gorgeous-And-Great-In-Bed-Macaulay"[12] I realised that the idea carried very little weight. Despite my new name, I still wasn't. Furthermore, the likes of Shaun Edwards and Henry Paul hadn't turned into mindless battling drones either. This argument was dying on its feet. Besides,

---

12 I didn't really do this. For all the good it would've done me I
    might as well have changed my name to "Bender In A Bun".

Leeds players hadn't grown horns, St Helens players hadn't become saintly and Bradford players hadn't started winning games by simply bull-dozing the opposition. Well, perhaps they had – but we shall call them the exception that proves the rule.

The only meaningful objection I could find to raise against the implementation of the "Warriors" label was the "Bender In A Bun" exception. There just didn't seem to be much point to it. It served no purpose. The "Disneyfication" of Wigan RLFC was neither necessary nor particularly beneficial. The town of Wigan was already famous primarily due to its rugby team. The very word "Wigan" was synonymous with success on the rugby pitch. The club would gain nothing more than a few lazy marketing short-cuts from the new branding.

While I could understand the vision for a bright new competition with teams whose names were nicknames accessible to all (because heaven only knows how much we have always needed to shake off the image of the M62 and its limited spectatorship) I just didn't see the point. Not with Wigan. Nor did I ever see those catchy nicknames dominating the names of the towns or the cities themselves. Even if I had become a fully-fledged, signed-up "Warriors" fan, I would not have afforded the same acceptance to the opposition teams. Who wants to be beating Rhinos when you could be beating Leeds?

In the end I was swayed by the large number of supporters who either wanted to be Warriors or who just didn't care as long as they were watching a team in cherry and white hoops playing at Central Park. This was the prevailing attitude that won the day. And in any case, the name "Warriors" isn't such a bad one. Especially when you consider the alternatives floating about at the time – Wigan Wizards, Wigan Knights, Wigan Peers, Wigan Pies...the mind boggles. And if the Warriors name still bothers you, spare a thought for the Wakefield supporters who were given a name that they couldn't actually say after more than two pints.

"Which team do you follow?"

"Wakefield Trintguht Wldncfmlknts."

Or something like that.

You could argue, though, that the prospect of the change in names slipped in largely under the radar of the Wigan worriers at a time when the rugby league community in general were still having twitchy kittens over the altogether more alarming issue of team mergers.

Immediately prior to the advent of Super League, a new, streamlined and far more competitive league (both on and off the pitch) seemed to demand the merging of numerous clubs. The name "Calder" springs to mind. I prefer not to appear too glib about this matter, because I know full well how much their teams and identities mean to the rugby league towns in this country. With the economic downturn of the 1980s and the wholesale closures of mines, mills and factories, in many cases their rugby league clubs were all that some of these communities had left. The survival of their rugby league teams was about far more than the upholding of tradition.

It was matter of pride, hope, salvation and the protection of their only form of escape from the indignity of daily existence. Nobody should mess with that, and I for one understood why the suggestion was met with such bile.

Mind you, at the same time, in a spectacularly hideous display of "I'm all right Jack-ness", I would have happily accepted the suggested mergers for the good of the game. This was because I was certain that Wigan could merge with Leigh, Chorley, Widnes, Warrington, Rochdale, Bradford, Hull, Leeds, London and Paris and we would have happily absorbed the lot of them into the successful, world famous rugby machine that was Wigan RLFC. Not St Helens, though. We wouldn't have wanted to absorb them. They'd have given us the runs. But we could have merged with all the rest and within a couple of seasons this conglomerated team would have been playing in cherry and white at Central Park under the name of Wigan and thrashing St Helens on a regular basis. I was right, too, if the examples of Shuddersfield Eagles and Gateshull Thundersharks[13] are anything to go by. A merger is, after all, just the traditional way of saying "hostile takeover."

As a club, we may have seemed impervious to the threats of mergers and to superficial changes of identity. Sadly, though, we couldn't quite have things all our own way and one of the most traditional aspects of Wigan RLFC did not survive long into the summer era. Sunday

---

13 Which, incidentally, would have been the best kids cartoon never made.

September 5th 1999 is a date that will remain forever imprinted on the minds of many Wigan supporters. It was on this day that we said a reluctant goodbye to our spiritual home, Central Park. For ninety eight years, almost to the day, that beautiful, radiant cherry and white ground had been an intrinsic part of the match-day experience. I always felt so comfortable at Central Park, where I sat for so many seasons in the same creaking wooden seat in the Douglas Stand. Such was my love for the ground that I completely failed to notice its short-comings. It wasn't until the penultimate season there, when I was working as a voluntary runner for Riverside Radio (housed in the Portacabin to the right of the scoreboard) that the reality dawned on me. The place was a mess. Walking in some time before the match, I had the opportunity to see the ground as it really was. With my view unobstructed by supporters, I surveyed the dilapidated stands, the crumbling terraces and the peeling paintwork, and I knew it was time to move on. This knowledge didn't make it any easier. It just helped me understand why change was necessary. I will always choose to remember Central Park full to the rafters on a sunny afternoon, with its perfect pitch and its bright colours. Had we stayed there much longer those memories might have been supplanted by ones of a stadium increasingly unfit for purpose. The final game there against St Helens was a wonderful occasion but I didn't linger in the way that so many did. At the end of the game I took a deep breath before affectionately patting that creaky wooden seat, and then I made my way out through the gates for the final time. That's what you have to do sometimes – move on with dignity and decisiveness.

My first experience of our new stadium left me feeling particularly horrified – I thought the concourse was grey, cavernous and lifeless. But now it is a special place in its own right, it just took a bit of time. I suspect that traditions always manage to rebuild themselves, given time. Experiences help too, and we've certainly had a few of those at the DW Stadium. Epic encounters, elation and heartbreak and the lifting of the league-leader's trophy have all gone some way to helping us bed in. As did the almighty fight to avoid relegation in 2006. It felt like Mission Impossible all over again, and it meant as much to the average Wigan fan as the winning of any trophy.

There was always something glorious about the play offs at the bottom the table. While the teams at the top of the table were gearing up for the big push, the teams at the bottom were going at it hammer and tongs in the superhuman effort to avoid the trapdoor. The sense of desperation that permeated these dogfights was almost tangible, adding a real sense of fraught brutality to the encounters. This anxious, vicious and desperate outbreak of rugby league warfare was what we called the relegation battle, and I have genuinely missed it. Traditionally it might not have offered the class evident in play off games, but in its place it served up lashings of vitriol and dogged determination. What the relegation battle lacked in polish it made up for in spit. The phrase "sudden death" seems to have been specially made for the battle between those teams at the foot of the table. When the prize was survival and the forfeit was to be cast down into the pit, who cared if the skills on show were not always of the highest quality? You could tell how much it meant just by looking into the eyes of the players and the fans. It was raw, it was emotional and it had real meaning. It was rugby league with its heart on its sleeve.

But suddenly it vanished. Another tradition fell by the wayside and in its place we were given the rather sterile franchise system. This simply hasn't been anywhere near as colourful, and supporters of many teams continually moaned about the demise of relegation and promotion. Now, of course, we know all about the new league system to be introduced in the 2015 season that will reinstate an element of promotion and relegation. To my surprise, though, I have to admit that I am rather hesitant in welcoming such a move.

In a world where the only certainty seems to be increasing financial uncertainty, the franchise system might just have proved to be the sport's saving grace. Since Super League began in 1996 we have seen a number of teams bounce repeatedly between the top tier and the lower division. Even illustrious clubs with great support (such as Wigan) have come perilously close to falling out of the bottom of the league. In the main, though, it was the same teams repeatedly dropping down and popping back up again. To their credit some of those clubs currently seem to have managed to achieve stability. Whether they would now be quite as stable if the threat of relegation had been continually hanging over them is another matter. I suspect not. If you are the team in the lower division who is destined to rise again, then you could really do with knowing about it nearer to the beginning of the season than the end. With the best will in the world you are probably going to have to completely restructure your playing staff. Some of your championship winning players simply won't be good enough for Super League. Others will not be prepared to abandon their jobs in order to take up full time contracts. The result? A mad scramble for players in the off-season. As it happens you probably end up picking up a large number of players from the team who pass you in the opposite direction as you move up. Without wishing to dwell on the calibre of these players, it is worth asking the question about the psychological impact of playing your career forever in the twilight zone between relegation and promotion.

Looking at it from the perspective of the team who is destined to be relegated; just what are you supposed to do? You are staring down the barrel of a significant loss of income and a subsequent loss of playing staff that will most likely have the effect of losing you a good few paying supporters. This isn't just a vicious circle. This is a nasty bastard vicious circle with knobs on[14]. You don't want to go there. So as soon as those warning signs appear, you

---

14 Poisonous knobs, no less.

throw more money into your team, accruing more debt that will need to be cleared at some point. Assuming you do manage to survive for another season in the top flight, then that is when those pigeons are going to come home to roost. And as they do, that vicious circle will be there again, flexing his knobs. Except this time you won't have the capital to buy your way out, just more debt to worry about when the inevitable happens.

Then there are the players. A career in rugby league is a short one. It might pay well for those at the top, but only for a limited time and there is always the potential for real uncertainty. We tend to forget that players have lives outside the sport, which inevitably means mortgages to pay and families to support. Relegation is more than a temporary inconvenience for some players, it can have serious repercussions.

The franchise system has allowed clubs to develop their financial plans over a more sensible length of time. Granted, three years is still not an adequate period to build your business plan on, but it is much better than not being able to think beyond a single season. Anything can invoke the threat of relegation – backroom issues, injury crises and even the threat of relegation itself. Over a single season these factors can prove critical, but they are far less likely to do so over a three year period. Rugby league clubs don't have the best track record when it comes to financial management, and it is right and proper for the sport to look at ways of affording them greater security.

It is true that there has always been an amount of

disgruntlement surrounding the licensing system, with a number of clubs repeatedly urging the RFL to review the situation, often with a return to promotion and relegation in mind. It is also true that many people were dead set against the new system simply because it was a new system. The knee-jerk antipathy to the franchise system is just like people who dismiss things like SATNAVs out of hand. People like my elderly neighbour who won't have it that SATNAVs are in any way useful. If anything, he would stoically maintain that they're just trouble, pure and simple. He's read about them in the Daily Mail, leading innocent drivers astray with that sexy but firm voice. The voice of the Navigatrix. And he just doesn't do sexy and firm, my elderly neighbour. Besides, he will tell you, there's something honourable about a good, old fashioned map-book. You know where you are with a map. Maps are safe. He'll be telling you this as he is driving along at 80mph, thumbing through the pages of a battered map book and steering with his feet. Then he will miss his junction, succumb to road rage, hurl the map aside and navigate by some mystical innate sense of lostness.

It's a poor way of finding your location, but he insists that it is better than using a SATNAV because...well, just because! I can't really fault him. For some reason it is an intrinsic part of the nature of humanity that we are drawn to chaos and uncertainty. Chaos and uncertainty is exactly what you get when Eric is succumbing to one of his map-rage incidents. To give him his due, it is certainly entertaining – providing you're not in a hurry to get somewhere and you happen to have a decent life insurance policy.

And that's the key point. Because among all that wild, chaotic, unpredictable madness there is always the solid security of an insurance policy to rely on.

Chaos is fun up to a point. It can be very engaging and entertaining to watch, but without the security, it is short term gain for long term pain. Those people who have been crying out for the return to promotion and relegation were simply giving air to their desire for chaos. And that's exactly what promotion and relegation is, with its ups and downs and its ins and outs. It is watchable but inevitably destructive chaos.

Admittedly, the argument that relegation battles give supporters something to turn up for is indeed a convincing one, but then, if Bradford's recent plight is anything to go by, so does financial mismanagement when it threatens your club's franchise. The franchise system may have had its faults but at least it is philosophically and morally sound. Sadly, the faults seem to have been allowed to bring the whole system down.

For all I know it may be extremely difficult to independently assess a club's financial viability. Perhaps, though, that wasn't the real problem. Perhaps the problem was that clubs were required to make self-assessments and submit them to the governing body. Or maybe the problem was that it was too easy to hide the smoking revolvers and blood-stained carpets of financial mismanagement from the governing body. Perhaps what the RFL really needed was a financial inspection team that was a bit more Columbo and a bit less Clouseau. That would've done it – a financial inspector who would suddenly turn around as he headed towards the exit, scratching his head in faux bafflement, to say "Just one more thing..."

Even better would have been for Sky to have got rid of the irritating purveyor of circular argument that is the "Super League Backchat" programme and replaced it with "CSI Super League Franchise". Then we could have had a hard-hitting fly-on-the-wall reality TV programme in which a team of franchise inspectors pay clubs unexpected visits, sift through their files and subject key personnel to "Apprentice" style interviews (or waterboarding, which is possibly less humiliating). The viewing public could then be asked to make their own decisions regarding the awarding of franchises through the time-honoured tradition of an interactive telephone vote.

As a system it would have been more transparent, which seems to be what most people desire. But it would also be less impartial. Which also seems to be what most people desire.

One of the reasons many people decried the franchise system was because they perceived it as being a false means of protecting the "expansion" clubs that lie beyond the game's heartlands. If this was really the case then I applaud the system even more. They might not be traditional, but we need those clubs. Catalans, the London Broncos and the Crusaders club (the latter two now sadly lost to the top flight) are to be cherished and nurtured. To allow them to fall by the wayside is the equivalent of playing safety-first rugby when you're winning by six points with twenty minutes left on the clock. Rugby League cannot be allowed to withdraw into itself, there is simply no future in that strategy. And while people have criticised the low numbers in attendance at the games involving those clubs, the fact is they are relatively new sporting clubs (yes, even the London club) in the process of putting down roots in a very competitive environment. How many well established professional rugby union clubs are currently enjoying financial success and security while retaining their prime location in the country's capital city?

I loved my trips to those expansion clubs more than any other, not just because London and Wrexham are closer to me than Wigan, but because I see something special in the game being played before those wide-eyed and optimistic supporters.

I'm very much aware that I've nailed my colours firmly to the mast of a ship that has already sunk. However, I am not entirely despondent. The influx of further money from Sky and the new league format will hopefully afford relegated clubs an easier transition. Perhaps Bradford and London will flourish in the lower league, and will one day return to the top flight with stronger resolve and firmer foundations. I hope so. And who knows – the Challenge Cup may still send me to places like London and Wales every so often.

Traditions are important. Whether they are the traditions that have held our sport together, or those more personal and individual traditions that we build into our own rugby routine, they become meaningful and full of value to us.

As such we should never simply abandon our traditions for the sake of change. To do so would be to lose our sense of identity. Nor should we seek to stick by them no matter what, because sometimes change is a good thing. It is difficult to choose a philosophical approach that would act as a foolproof and infallible system of choosing which traditions to retain and which ones to attempt to replace. The choice would always be between the Kant-like emphasis on duty (in this case the duty owed to the past) that stresses the need to do what is right, just for the sake of doing right (which would see us sticking steadfast to our tried and tested ways of old), or alternatively to dismiss the past and focus solely on the potential consequences of actions. The second alternative seems to be the more pioneering approach and the one that takes the changing nature of the world around us directly into account. But can we really afford to ride roughshod over our illustrious past?

Perhaps the answer lies in a more utilitarian approach, and with the principle of the hedonic calculus. This method looks primarily at consequences in order to ascertain the amount of happiness a course of action might generate, measuring it in terms of intensity, duration, fruitfulness and extent. But it also includes purity in the equation. In rugby league terms, purity can be considered the measure of how much an action takes our historical and traditional values into account. It is a compromise weighted in favour of the pioneering approach, but it still takes into account our time-honoured customs. This would appear to be the most sensible way forward for the Wiganosopher.

As it happens, there is good news for those of us who sit at our seats in the DW Stadium wearing our lucky underpants, munching on our Cadbury's Double Deckers and trying to persuade the person next to us (who we may or not know) that change is a good thing. We have an ace up our sleeve. Rugby league has always been a pioneering sport, right from the outset. It was born out of a pioneering spirit, breaking away from the Union as it did all those years ago. Since then we have led the way in so many different areas. Thirteen players, world cups, summer rugby, video referees – the list goes on and on. Our tradition is important, but the spirit of revolution is an inherent part of our tradition. As fans and spectators who have the natural tendency to be curmudgeonly and unyielding at times, we should continuously remind ourselves of this most important of time-honoured rugby league traditions.

"I am Wigan till I die. Viva La Revolution!"

A FAMILY AFFAIR

When you flick through the pages of your match-day programme, stood in the concourse, with your pie in one hand and your pint between your knees, you will probably miss the most important bit in there. Your first instinct will be to find out who the referee is. Following this you will then peruse the team sheet (not that it means anything these days), before seeking out the comments of the coach and then the chairman. This seems to be the agreed programme-reading routine adopted by most fans. Any further spare moments prior to kick off and during the half-time break can be used to delve into the many other fascinating and entertaining articles and interviews contained between the covers of the programme. But even then you would probably still miss it. The important bit that you're missing will be tucked away somewhere at the back – on those pages that you read on the toilet some time during the following the week. It's in there somewhere, in a smaller font and neatly tucked away. It is nestled beneath the bit that tells you exactly what to do in the event of an emergency (always handy when you're on the toilet). Below this disaster-scenario protocol there are clear guidelines regarding foul and abusive behaviour. And then you've found it, because it is here that it is clearly stated that rugby league is a family sport.

This is one of the two things that I have always been told about rugby league. Firstly, that it is the "Greatest Game" and secondly that it is a "Family Sport".

In my mind there is no question that this sport of ours is indeed the greatest game of all. The evidence for this is entirely overwhelming and anybody who says otherwise is clearly suffering from some form of delusional mindset.

Without looking, I also wholeheartedly leap onto the "Family Sport" bandwagon too, because…well, because it just feels right.

That's why.

It just feels right. When I am sitting comfortably in my seat at the match surrounded by people who are unquestionably members of families. Yes, it does just feel right.

But is it right? Beyond the rather glib observation that the vast majority of supporters are members of families, is it correct to label rugby league as a "family sport" and if so, by what standards or criteria?

I know why I want it to be right. I love the very words, "A Family Sport". Those words send shivers up and down my spine, followed by a sudden, radiant burst of warm, glowing pride. And why shouldn't they? For the life of me I cannot think of a greater endorsement for a sport. To be referred to as a family sport is the ultimate accolade, because what is "family"? It is love, care, acceptance and forgiveness. It is united against the outside world. It is closer than close – an unspoken bond that demands unquestioning, unfaltering loyalty. It is brave and it is blind faith (by far the most ferociously potent flavour of faithfulness). All of these things seem to sum up my passion for the Wigan Warriors perfectly.

Once I've pulled my replica shirt over my hairy gut, made the one hundred and sixty mile journey north and merged with the other fans entering the stadium, that is exactly what it feels like – a family.

But this is just family at its best. What about family at its worst? What is that like? Bickering and back-biting, impatient and inconsiderate, obstinate and stubborn. And airing its dirty washing on the Jeremy Kyle Show. Lets face it, rugby league can be like that sometimes too.

Of course, you can interpret a label like "The Family Sport" in a number of very different ways. At its most basic level it refers to a game that the whole family can enjoy together. This alone is gold dust (just look at the value the TV industry places on programmes that the whole family can watch together). As a parent, the question "can I bring my kids here?" is usually foremost in my mind wherever I go. I want my children to share in the most exciting experiences of my life. But I also want them to feel safe, secure and comfortable. I personally would have no qualms about bringing them to Wigan with me to see a match. And there you'd have it – two ready-made fans of the future. The next decade's season ticket holders. From a financial point of view being a family sport is of paramount importance. From a dad's point of view it is just as vital, because it might just placate my wife.

Ah yes, my wife.

I'll be circumspect. My wife doesn't understand me. In particular she doesn't understand me when I refer to rugby league as a "family sport". Upon hearing those words her reaction is quite markedly different to mine. She laughs like a drain. To her, it is the "anti-family sport".

She is of the opinion that our children are too young to attend rugby matches. Sadly I have to admit that she is in fact correct, they really are too young. Like me, she is a teacher. Unlike me, she hasn't blagged her way through her career. She knows stuff. She knows, for instance, that attention span is measured in minutes by the age of the child plus five. I didn't know about that. My system for measuring their attention spans was rather different – I was measuring them in sets of six. And, whichever system I use, I have to concede that neither of my children is ready to sit through a whole match yet. My youngest, bless him, wouldn't get as far as the first play the ball before his attention shifted to his next fix of breast milk. Whereas, by means of a comparison, these days I can go as far as five drives and a kick before I start thinking about breasts (unless Lee Briers is in attendence, in which case I am thinking about them for the whole of the match[15]).

In a few years time, though, when my offspring are able to sit through the whole game without resorting to numerous toilet trips just to keep them busy, I will be able to enjoy guilt-free rugby for the first time in many years. Rugby without the fear of incurring the wrath of a Mrs Macaulay who has had to look after the children in my absence – I do like the sound of that.

Alas, my wife's lack of understanding is not solely down to the current age of our children. There are other barriers between us.

She's from Bath. To be precise, she's from a nice little village on the outskirts of that beautiful spa town.

The cultural gulf between the son of a Wigan vicar and a girl from the rural south west is not unbridgeable. But there a few things that won't make it across. It became clear from the earliest days that my love of rugby league had fallen down the gap. Along with my ear ring.

While there were some promising signs during our initial courtship, when she even attended the occasional game, these signs evaporated literally as soon as the

---

15 This is not a slur against the character of Mr Briers. Rather it is due to an associate of mine from Warrington claiming to know "for a fact" that Mr Briers' team mates referred to him as "Bitch-tits" as a term of endearment. Other things this person claimed to know "for a fact" included the "fact" that infamous Yorkshire prop Ryan Bailey and our former second row Ian Bailey are brothers. Twins, no less.

honeymoon period ended. When a woman finds a man to be unique, interesting and, above all, the special one who is destined for her (presumably exactly because of his unique and interesting character traits) then she shows her intention to commit through a subtle process that makes it clear to everybody that he is "the one". She sets about changing him. Soon after the mysterious nocturnal disappearance of my ear ring, I began to wear my Wigan replica shirts less and less. I can't remember ever making this decision, it just sort of happened. Suddenly I wasn't attending parties and social events in my rugby shirts. They became just for "game days and exercise". So just game days, really.

At the same time, her tolerance level for all things rugby league related suddenly bottomed out. No longer would she sit and listen to my anecdotes about the 1995 Challenge Cup Final and the night I met Shaun Edwards and his dad in a car park in the Lake District. Her final attendance at a rugby match was the 2000 Challenge Cup Final between Bradford and Leeds at Murrayfield, it was the day after I proposed to her. Basically, she agreed to marry me and she hasn't been to a game since. In fact, since then her views about rugby league have become more and more entrenched.

It is no family game to her. It is the thing that keeps me away from the family. It is the obstacle that threatens to undermine social events, family occasions and holidays. It is the beast that I put before her beauty.

I have, over the years, become accustomed to her

attitude and I would go as far as to say that I understand it. I now know and recognise that slight tensing of her facial muscles when, as she is arranging some obscure family social event, she stops herself, looks at me and says:

"There isn't a match that day, is there?"

When she says that, I already know the answer. It's "no". Because even if there is, there isn't for me. Otherwise there would be flouncing and utterances of words like "typical" and "selfish". I can immediately recognise when it is not worth arguing. On those other occasions, when I sense some leeway in the offing, then I must enter into negotiation. Such negotiations are emotional minefields, devoid of logic and laced with strange, bizarre statements of hers that seem meaningless and surreal. Things like...

"IS IT AN IMPORTANT GAME?"

A question like this is deeply troubling and points to a complete lack of understanding as to why somebody goes to watch a rugby game. How do you even begin to answer it? Is there ever an unimportant game? Perhaps it can be argued that sometimes, because of the vagaries of the league table, the points available for a win will not make any difference to the final league positions. But does this make the game unimportant? Surely for a spectator the important thing is to watch and enjoy the contest. Just being there – being part of it – is in itself important. In this respect even a pre-season friendly match against an amateur, fledgling side from Torquay would be important.

Now, the chances of my wife understanding this are quite remote, so here is the best way to answer this particular question:-

Adopt a serious look. Nod gravely.
"Yes, it is," you say.

In other words, you blag it.

And hopefully she won't ask any more questions about it, such as "why is it important?"

"IF YOU'RE SO SURE YOU'RE GOING TO WIN/ LOSE THEN WHY BOTHER WATCHING?"

Oh, how I despair of this particular question! This is the tell-tale sign that she has completely failed to grasp the very essence of my relationship with the rugby. Knowing that your team will win is one thing, watching them do it is quite another. In fact that is the whole point, isn't it? That is why successful teams gather larger crowds (apart from Huddersfield who have recently mastered the curious art of marrying success and thin attendance figures). It is because you want to go and watch and be part of that success. There is something wonderfully cathartic and uplifting about watching Wigan totally dismantle another team, even if you knew it was going to happen. Especially if that team has done the same to us in previous seasons, because no game stands on its own or in isolation. There is always a history. Each and every game played against every other team is just another battle in the war. One day they may beat Wigan again, so it is vital that you enjoy the win when you can.

As for being confident of a loss, you still go because it is important to display loyalty and also because there is always that slight, elusive chance that Wigan will turn the tables on the opposition and beat them. And you would not want to miss out on that. How could you – those games are the stuff of legend. Who can forget the 2003 Good Friday showdown between Wigan and St Helens? The result was unexpected and against the odds – a totally uplifting event. That's completely why we bother watching.

But, to put it into perspective, in language that she might possibly have a chance of understanding, the best thing to do is throw the same question back at her.

"But if you already know that there will be one obligatory tragic death which will then be overcompensated for by a series of unfeasibly fortuitous resolutions to all the other problems, all of which will be relayed to you using dialogue a six year old could have written – then why do you bother watching 'Downton Abbey'?"

That is sure to help.

"YOU'LL JUST HAVE TO RECORD IT AND WATCH IT LATER."

The notion that a televised match can be recorded and viewed later on without losing any of the enjoyment is entirely false. It just isn't the same. The reason it isn't the same is because you are simply not "living" the event; the chronological distance between yourself and the game serves as an emotional buffer, divorcing you from the passion and excitement. Regardless of whether you know the result or not, the fact that you are not experiencing the event second by second along with everybody else nullifies the entire thing.

There is little point in invoking the "Downton Defence" here – she often does record Downton Abbey and watches it later. Instead it is perhaps better to use a more fitting example from real life.

"How about I don't come with you to your parents' house this afternoon? In my place you can take this photograph of me and then I can phone them later and tell them what I would have said if I had been there at the time."

The logic is impeccable and will enable her to understand the value of a live event (although part of me does suspect that, should I ever summon up the courage to actually say this, then I wouldn't personally be a "live event" for very much longer).

"YOU DON'T HAVE TO SHOUT AT THE TV, THEY CAN'T HEAR YOU!"

Here I am guilty as charged, I'm afraid. You might call it overcompensation, or pent up frustration at not being able to attend personally; you might even call it boorish drunkenness from the safety of my own living room. In fact you can call it what you like. The simple truth is that I am often far more vociferous when watching a game on the telly than I am at the match.

I don't know why. I just am. For one thing, I cannot watch a televised game while seated. I have to roam about the living room, beer in hand, providing a running commentary. Throughout the game I also persist in roaring loudly enough to ensure the whole village has some idea of how a match is going.

I suppose it is true that there is more than a "slight" element of overcompensation. Not being there, not sitting alongside my father and sharing in the event with him does mar the experience somewhat. If I'm honest I also feel a little bit like I've let him down. So, like a player who has just given away a silly penalty, I put in the extra effort. It makes me feel better.

By whipping myself up into such a frenzy I also ensure that the game is more of an event for me, rather than just something I happen to be passively watching on TV. I want to feel involved. I want to feel part of it. I want the neighbours to look through my living room windows to see me shouting my head off and bouncing on the sofa. I want them to say "Oh look, Macaulay's getting quite involved in the rugby." I want the world to understand how much the whole thing means to me. Sadly, more often than not when I am watching on TV, I am alone. I don't have a friend or companion to share in the ups and downs with. So I do my best to share them very loudly with the rest of the village.

I like to think of this as outreach work. If the residents of a small village nestled between Cirencester and Cricklade know that Wigan are playing, because they can hear my screams carried upon the evening air, then I'm doing my bit for the expansion of rugby league.

None of which remotely interests my wife. There really is no excuse for waking the children up and so I am left with only one course of action.

"I'm sorry, it won't happen again."

It will.

At least I know that my wife's antipathy towards the game is not down to contempt for the sport itself. At one point I was worried that she actually preferred rugby union and was guilty of the prejudices that I so despise. However, she assures me that this is not the case. It could be any sport or recreational activity. She dislikes them all equally, especially the ones that make me behave like a yobbish, loud-mouthed cheering boor and a selfish fool who rejects his own family.

The bottom line is this: she is the most faithful,

supportive and loving woman I could ever hope to have met. I have never doubted her commitment to me and I never will.

Ever.

Yet there was one occasion when I felt truly betrayed by her. A time when she hurt me so much that she might as well have stabbed me repeatedly in the back of the head with a rusty spoon. That's how painful it was.

It was on the morning of the 2003 rugby union world cup final. Her parents were staying over at our house that week and they were in the living room watching England take on the Wallabies. I could just about tolerate this behaviour, although I wasn't entirely comfortable with it. My discomfort became heightened as Sarah (despite her claim to be disinterested) would keep popping in to look at the television. I admit that this niggled me, but I could cope with it because I knew that occasionally she had (albeit accidentally) looked at the television when rugby league was on. So it sort of equalled itself out. But the betrayal came on the 100th minute when England scored the drop goal that won them the game. And my wife cheered. She leapt to her feet and she actually showed genuine excitement, in the form of a loud and prolonged cheer. I was devastated.

She'd never done that for Wigan. It was like she was going behind my back with Jonny Wilkinson.

All these years on and I still have difficulty with that memory. At the time, I bottled it up and kept it all in. I didn't want to make a song and dance about it. Don't worry, I told myself, you'll get your own back one day. I did, too.

My revenge came earlier this year as she drove my four year old daughter through Bath. They passed a Bath RU training pitch on their way out of the city and, upon seeing the rugby posts, my daughter became excited and asked her mother "Are we in Wigan?"

Victory is mine!

There are other reasons why my wife might be justified in suggesting that rugby has a largely negative effect on family life. It makes me grumpy.

On occasions that are too numerous to mention, a drastic loss at the hands of a team such as Leeds, Warrington or St Helens has instigated a significant change in my temperament. The result is markedly similar to the effect Gamma Radiation had on Bruce Banner. It turns me into "The Incredible Sulk".

I strop about, grunting like an obstinate teenager, throwing my toys out of my pram in all directions and mumbling insane comments about how it is time to give up my season ticket. To my regret, there have even been times when my petulant demeanour has upset my children. This idiotic and puerile behaviour does nothing for family cohesion and actually threatens the bond of the family unit. I sometimes become exasperated at my family's criticisms of my tendency to shout at the telly while watching rugby. Sadly, I suspect the reason my young children are so perturbed by this is because they cannot forget those few occasions when I have reacted very badly to losses. They have seen me spectacularly lose my temper over things they simply can't understand. This unfathomable transformation from cheerful, loving and devoted father into a howling beast must have terrified them. There is no excuse, and no apology can ever quite expunge the worry I have caused them.

I must simply remember that, at the end of the day, rugby is just rugby. Family, on the other hand, is family.

Sometimes rugby can be family too. Sometimes being a rugby league devotee is akin to being a member of a very large extended family. For instance, there is always a little thrill of pleasure to be gleaned from seeing cars on the motorway that are decorated with the flags and colours of Super League teams. The pleasure of such a sight is made even greater when you are beyond the boundaries of the rugby league heartlands. I love to see them – those rugby league cars. Regardless of whichever team their owner might support, there is always a nod of acceptance and approval from the driver. A sort of fleeting acknowledgement of common ground and of a shared interest. They don't have to do it. There is nothing forcing them to make the effort. Fellow Wigan supporters might be expected to give a little wave as they drive by, but there is no reason to expect supporters of teams like Castleford or Wakefield to make that sort of gesture. And yet they always do. This, of course, is almost entirely down to the "family" nature of the game we choose to follow. The supporters of other teams generally do give a little wave to me. They do this despite the fact that they know and I know (and they know that I know) that deep down inside they really resent the Wigan sticker on my car. Which is why I find it necessary to overtake them at any cost.

After all, there are standards to maintain. And I can't let some supporter of a lesser team beat me and my Fiat Doblo. Once they've been overtaken, if they've got any sense they'll stay overtaken. Sometimes, though, they don't have any sense. Sometimes they throw down the gauntlet and initiate motorway dogfights that can last the whole length of the British Isles.

I will never forget one particular occasion when I was leaving London on the West Way, and a St Helens supporter steadfastly refused to stay overtaken. Looking through my window as he accelerated past me, I recognised the same look of crazed determination in his eyes that I knew he would see in my own. So I put my foot down and made sure that I shot him a triumphant glance as I hurtled by.

Seconds later he was returning the glance through my driver's side window. What followed was a rugby league themed game of vehicular leap-frog all the way up the M40. The gauntlet had been thrown down and both of us meant business. And every time I caught a glimpse of him it was like looking at an alternative St Helens version of myself staring back at me. Different to me, and yet the same as me. Sure enough, he even had the same wide-eyed, panic-consumed children in the back seat as me, and the same screaming wife in the front trying to hit him with the map book. Like a mirror image, it was. The same but different.

I missed my junction that afternoon. I did not do this by accident but through the sheer bloody-minded determination that I wasn't going to bottle out of the contest before he did. I chased him all the way to the West Midlands before he eventually turned off the motorway and I was able to declare myself the victor. I then had to come off at the next junction, do a U-turn and backtrack sixty miles down the motorway.

Oh, how I love our family game.

I love that we understand each other, regardless of whichever team we happen to support. What could be more family-like? We actively choose our friends, bonding with those who best fulfil our exacting criteria. Family, on the other hand is like a lucky dip. You get what you get. Usually you get at least one domineering matriarch, cousins whom you fear and pity in equal measure and one totally unhinged uncle[16]. The thing is, though, that despite their various faults and flaws, they're family. You understand them. You don't necessarily "like" them, but family love and understanding goes a long way.

Conversely, family has to go a long way to jeopardise that feeling of love and understanding. But it does happen, even in rugby league.

---

16   In rugby league terms, the domineering matriarch is probably the NRL. The shifty cousins are definitely Leigh fans, and as for the unhinged uncle – Gary Schofield.

Following the Dave Whelan takeover, I was actually quite enthusiastic about our club's future. I saw the renewed affiliation with JJB as a very positive development. JJB was a name recognised right across the country, there was even a branch near to my (then) Great Missenden home and it felt like, through JJB, the Wigan RL family was opening its arms and reaching out to embrace me. Buoyed by this sense of belonging, I strolled happily into the Aylesbury branch of JJB and asked the store manager where in her shop I would find the official Wigan replica shirts for the coming season.

"We don't have them," she replied, with all the charm and warmth of a dead snake.

"Oh," I said, trying to hide my surprise and to remain positive, "could you tell me when you'll be getting them in, please?"

"This is Aylesbury, sir. We will not be getting any Wigan rugby shirts in stock in the foreseeable future."

"How about the unforeseeable future?" I joked.

She checked her diary. "No."

"In that case, could you order one from another JJB store?"

"No, we couldn't be sure of finding a Wigan shirt in any other JJB store," she countered.

"I'm pretty sure they'd have them in JJB Wigan. You see, you are our team's main shirt sponsors…"

"You are mistaken, sir," she snapped, "we don't sponsor your team, we *own* your team."

And I really, really wanted to think of a sharp and witty

retort that would reacquaint her with her true position in society, but none came to mind. Instead I just asked her if she'd be having any personal involvement in the hospitality arrangements at the club. She couldn't tell me. She couldn't even tell me about any new signings she might have been privy to, which, I informed her, was the least I would expect from one of the club's owners. What she could tell me was that unless I made a purchase, she would have me removed from the premises.

Wigan RL, through JJB, might have been reaching out to me, but not to embrace me as much as to flick the Vs at me. I didn't really feel like a part of the family as I left the Aylesbury branch of JJB that afternoon. I felt more like a prat. And the warmth I had felt for the JJB label – a warmth fostered by my father's allegiance to a sports shop in his home town, and by our frequent visits to that shop in my youth – evaporated there and then.

Family can be delicate, despite its deep roots, mainly because the feelings associated with family are so strong and overwhelming. Thinking back on my own earlier memories, they speak of comfort and of vulnerability in equal measure. Those trips to the JJB sports shop, hand in hand with my father remind me of feeling quite exposed as I was conveyed into an alien world of which I had little understanding, while also feeling secure in the protection of my father. Where the two contrasting emotions meet, there is the potential for turbulence and upset. This is what childhood and growing up is all about – that emotional mixture is a feeling I recall as vividly as my first taste of

Uncle Joes Mintballs, my Saturday afternoons at Wigan roller rink and my days as a pupil at St Peter's Primary School, Hindley.

Back in those days the playground was often buzzing with talk of the rugby team. It wasn't conversation supported by any kind of real knowledge, more a basic way of defining who we were and where we were from. We were from Wigan. Where they play rugby. And this was our extended Wigan family.

These days, though, most students I teach tend to end up supporting St Helens or Leeds (apart from back in 1998 when almost every pupil in the Misbourne School, Great Missenden, became an overnight Sheffield Eagles fanatic). I like this – it is their way of making me feel part of their family. Let's face it, they are never going to actually support Wigan. That would be an altogether too sycophantic response to having a Wigan fan as a teacher. It would be openly inviting a sound beating behind the bike sheds for crawly bum licking of the worst order. Besides, I wouldn't want them to support Wigan as it would make me feel uncomfortable – it would feel worryingly like they were taking the first step on the road to Stalkerville. But I do appreciate the way that so many of them make the effort to support a team that could well at some point break my heart by giving Wigan a good thrashing. It is their way of saying "we like you enough to show an interest in what causes you pain," and with teenagers that's about as good as it gets.

It also enables us to talk to each other like human beings every once in a while, even if it is about how badly my team were beaten. Teachers need that sort of interaction with students and, quite frankly, it doesn't happen nearly enough.

One of the most moving moments of my career to date came towards the end of my final year at the Friary School in Lichfield. I had one of those Year Eleven groups that are quite often described as being "full of characters" (this is the phrase generally used by those members of the teaching profession who can cope – it's "full of shits" by those who can't). One of those characters was a young man called Danny. He had a reputation for being a particularly accident-prone "joy rider" of other people's cars. During our final lesson of the year, as I was threatening to knee-cap anybody in the group who failed to include technical terms in their exam answers, Danny stood up and presented me with a nicely wrapped gift. I was rather startled by this uncharacteristic display of affection. I pulled away the wrapping paper to find a replica Wigan home shirt with my name and lucky number on the back – a gift that would have cost something in region of £45. It transpired that, perhaps with a little "persuasion" from Danny, the class had clubbed together to buy the shirt online. I went from startled to speechless in zero seconds. Looking back, I suppose I should have seen it coming – all those questions about what my favourite number was, how to spell my surname properly and, most pointedly, that curious exchange about my size.

"God, sir, you're fat – I bet you're a size L aren't you? Or maybe an XL?"

I thought they were just being cheeky. In retrospect, I should've been a bit more honest with them – that shirt is a really snug fit.

Looking at this class of characters, I held up my new shirt and thanked them from the very bottom of my heart, before wiping away the tears, putting the shirt to one side and resuming my spiel about the sort of pain I inflict on individuals who don't mention "the sanctity of life" in the ethics question. At this moment the door opened and Mrs F walked into the room. She was a recent addition to the department who would be taking over most of my groups when I left and she was very eager to win the hearts and minds of the students. A bit too eager, really.

With me openly threatening them, and the Wigan shirt on the desk beside me, she saw her chance. Oblivious to the act of generosity that had just occurred, she made her way over to the desk where the shirt lay. She picked it up, pushed me aside and, without a word, made a big deal of dropping it onto the floor and then (in slow-motion, no less) proceeded to wipe her feet all over it. Mrs F then looked triumphantly to the class for some show of approval. But deathly silence had fallen upon the room and all she was getting was gaping mouths and wide eyes. Without missing a beat, Danny smiled sweetly at her and asked, "Miss, which is your car?"

Stupidly, she told him.

The classroom can be a hard world. I was part of the

family and Mrs F wasn't. Even indirectly, being a Wigan supporter has made it easier for people to accept me. Not because of Wigan per se – these kids knew little of Wigan's glorious history or of the days when we were the most famous team in England. They only knew that I supported a particular team in a particular sport and that was enough for them. They recognised in me a human trait that they understood and related to.

If only my wife was as easily appeased.

My father assures me that the secret in dealing with wives lies in timing, in much the same way as it does with a good piece of attacking rugby. Knowing exactly what to say is one thing, knowing exactly when to say it is quite another. Unfortunately, I haven't proved to be much good at either. Generally speaking, I tend to blurt out my expectations of attending matches at the most inappropriate times.

When it comes to family, it is always important to retain a sense of what is and what isn't appropriate. I remember there were whispers and rumours that the Super League's much maligned £00.00 sponsorship deal with Stobart in 2012 was the only offer left on the table after the RFL rejected a deal with a gambling company. If this is true then it must surely have been a strategic decision taken on the basis of rugby league's reputation as a family game. What a statement to make! I haven't a clue how much money would have been involved, but to turn down hard cash at a time of global economic meltdown sounds like pure lunacy. Conversely, it does demonstrate the importance that our game places on its family status. This is a bold and admirable trait. Embracing more lucrative sponsorship deals with breweries or bookies might not directly harm our children or even our reputation, but it would leave us open to the accusation of hypocrisy. Think of soccer and how hollow and cynical the likes of Sepp Blatter sound when they are countering accusations of institutional racism and homophobia within the sport. There but for the grace of God goes rugby league.

Yes, these are hard times and our rugby league family has taken some serious financial hits. Money truly is too tight to mention and that's not going to change in a while. Perhaps accepting a few bob from companies like Foxy Bingo and even Mecca and Coral (as indeed Wigan now have) is the way forward. It might well give us a comfortable short-term boost, after all. But what does it profit a sport to gain the whole world, and forfeit its soul? It is a fine line to tread. We may take the cash and alleviate the financial suffering of our clubs, only to risk alienating the general public to a degree that our game, unlike soccer, could not withstand. We really are existing on the raggedy edge.

We are not the Coral Wigan Warriors. The difference between a club's main shirt sponsor and the Super League sponsors, whoever they are, is that they will have the luxury of prefixing our flagship competition. People who are unaware of the nature and tenets of our game will make a value judgement based on this. The best sponsors are always the judgement-neutral ones.

Whatever the future brings, though, it is worth remembering three things. Firstly, in general amongst the non-followers, the image of a family game has stuck. They may see us as quirky, northern and odd, but they are aware of our strength. They know that while we look after our own, all are welcome and made to feel comfortable at our stadia.

Secondly, we are a family sport and when things get tough, family is where you find the strength to survive.

Thirdly, if you really are that worried about money, just have a quick look at the debt accrued by the Latics during their years in the Premiership. That should cheer you up.

I don't know whether or not we will sacrifice a little of our soul for the sake of financial gain. I don't know whether or not those responsible for steering our game through murky waters are prepared to jeopardise our reputation as a family game. What I do know is this – family is strength.

Family is the proverbial teabag – you put it in hot water and it just gets stronger. Family has the capacity to repel the onslaught of the world outside, but only when it plays to its strengths. Sometimes the rest of the world doesn't matter because the family can weather any storm. To do this it needs to be true to its core values, holding them dear even if at times it does have to resort to desperate measures. If it came to it, I would sell my own soul for my family. I would do this because I know that I am willing to pass into hell for a heavenly cause.

Rugby league may have to make a few deals with the devil in the years ahead, but providing we all remember the importance of the years behind, our family will prevail.

Having skirted around any real attempt to define what "family" is, beyond the biological aspect of shared genetic material, it is perhaps pertinent at this point to consider a couple of suggestions from more learned philosophers.

Matt Groening, creator of The Simpsons, informs us that families are "about love overcoming emotional torture." This would seem to sum up the nature of the rugby league family quite succinctly. Every game is a cauldron of emotional torture and one of the things that makes it tolerable (and even makes attendance a necessity) is the sense that you are a member of a wider family. You will only put yourself through that hell for your family, and having your family with you gives you the inner strength to cope with potential heartbreak.

You see your closest relatives on the loo. You watch them rise and fall, you pick them up and you wipe them down. You nurse them through their sickness and their darkest days – and it is hard work. You feel little in the way of resentment, though. Instead you feel love.

You grumble about them, mind you. You know their faults and flaws better than most and they hurt you and niggle away at you. But with family you're always ready to forgive for the sake of a moment of pure warmth and joy.

Warmth and joy. Those moments I spend, side by side with my dad in WS6, when Wigan have just scored. That is the love that overcomes emotional torture.

My favourite family quotation, however, comes from the American writer Kendall Hailey who came up with this gem:-

"The great gift of family life is to be intimately acquainted with people you might never even introduce yourself to, had life not done it for you."

When I gaze across the sea of cherry and white attired individuals in attendance at any game, I feel bound to them in some deep and abiding way. I am comfortable in their presence and feel compelled to embrace them (I mean this metaphorically, by and large). It is true to say that, without the connection of rugby league and of Wigan in particular, I would have no such compulsion. In fact many of these individuals are people I would probably have actively avoided had it not been for our shared membership of this family. My existence would have lacked something very special had this been the case, for many of these people have enriched my life in inestimable ways. I'm so glad that we are family.

There is one occasion I remember with particular fondness. It was back in 2010 when, having suffered a particularly nasty injury in a cycling accident, I was unable to drive up to the rugby match. Instead I took the train from Kemble – a gruelling experience in itself, made worse by the discomfort, pain and physical ineptitude of having my arm strapped up around my shoulder. Needless to say, the train was late.

Meanwhile, up in Wigan, my father was having kittens. Here is a man who likes to be in his seat at least an hour before kick-off, now pacing the concourse nervously as the start of the game drew ever nearer. The thought that he might have to miss the first few minutes in order to pick me up at the station did not sit well with him. Then there were the issues of getting back, parking and dragging my hobbling lump of a bruised body back to the stadium. Eventually he bumped into a gentleman employed by the club and informed him of our predicament. This was a true gentleman, as it happens. And this gentleman duly found my father a free parking space at the entrance to the club and held it for him while my dad raced from the stadium to collect me from the station. When we finally returned this gentleman was still waiting for us, he allowed us to park and ushered us in through the main entrance, just as the team were making their way past us into the tunnel. I'll never forget what that man did for us. I didn't know him and I'd never met him before or since, but he was definitely a true gentleman, and I remember his name – it was Keith Mills. How did that kindness make me feel?

It made me feel like family.

OFF-SEASONAL
AFFECTIVE DISORDER

Seasonal Affective Disorder is alive and well and living in my head. After twenty years I must now accept that my overwhelming tendency towards listless misery between the months of November and February is down to something more than blind coincidence. But it is not a weather thing. It's a rugby thing. Or, more to the point, it's a lack-of-rugby thing.

The weather is bad enough. The onset of winter heralds the beginning of the bitter end. As the month of November withers away and perishes, the gloom of December unfolds around us. The sense of age and mortality is tangible in the ether. Dawn appears each day only after a terrible struggle, its birth increasingly painful and laborious. The days, now shrouded in darkness, battle against the heartless clasp of the cold and the fog. Finally, the life is choked out of each of them before they have ever really lived. Victorious night rolls in to smother their prematurely dead remains. The stench of death hangs in the dark, cold, still air.

Some people, apparently, can get a bit miserable during the winter months. This is probably the reason why we throw practically every festival we've got at the winter. Halloween, Bonfire Night and Christmas are all there in an attempt to cheer us up a bit during the darkest days of the year.

Then there is New Year's Eve when I'm never entirely sure what I'm celebrating. To be honest, I don't know whether I should be rejoicing in the end of the previous, miserable year, or celebrating the fact that there is a new year on its way with a whole load of new miseries to celebrate and rejoice in. Not that it bothers me too much. I usually just get very drunk, fall over and wake up the next morning with an almighty hangover. At which point I start on my new year's resolutions – the first one usually being not to get quite so drunk next year.

Perhaps the answer is that I should be celebrating a little bit of everything. A little bit of relief that the old year is over, a little bit of appreciation for the great moments that the year gave me and a little bit of excitement at what the future might hold. I suppose that is what I should be celebrating at the stroke of midnight on New Year's Eve. But the truth is that I don't give it too much thought. It is only actually one of a number of new years that I experience in any one given year, and it is not really the most important.

Being a teacher, there is another end of year that occupies me far more than New Year's Eve. In fact it has pretty much taken up residence in my mind and dominated in my entire lifestyle. The last week in July is the end of the school year and the start of a six week long incessant sigh of relief. The frolics of New Year's Eve seem rather half-hearted by comparison. September then signals the start of a new year – a time when I am so refreshed and eager that I am almost of the opinion that I like my job.

But just to muddy the waters a little further, there is another new year lurking somewhere in the middle of the school year. As a head of faculty, I have a budget to mismanage. The financial year ends in April – a month I am always grateful for. The new year that follows gives me the chance to replenish my stock of board pens and lower the official threat level of what I like to call SBA (School Bursar Attack). The thought of not having to wake up alongside a horse's head pinned to an internal memo from the school finance office is far more pleasurable than waking up with a hangover on New Year's Day.

Of course, there is one more new year within the year – the start of the new rugby season.

This is a day to be warmly welcomed, particularly after the long, seemingly endless hell on earth of the dark, winter off-season. As a continuously travelling supporter, you might think I would be glad of the rest. You'd think the off-season would be a welcome break.

A break from the indignity of bump'n'grind in a dusty cupboard half way through lesson six on a Friday afternoon. I go in dressed in my suit and, after violently thrashing around in the dark for ten minutes, emerge in jeans and rugby shirt. And every week I look expectantly at my class of vegetating year eleven students, waiting for them to be amazed and astounded by my Superman-esque transformation. And every week, without fail, they don't notice.

Then there's the mad dash from the classroom to the car park. Pupils can vacate the premises pretty quickly on a Friday afternoon, clambering over bins, furniture and teachers as they do so. But I can do it quicker. Clambering over pupils as they clamber over bins, furniture and teachers. Leaping into my Fiat Doblo like the Dukes of Hazzard probably would if they were forty-something teachers on their way to the match in a cheap MPV. And what follows is the monumental Cirencester-to-Wigan rally, avoiding the M6 at all costs. Pedal to the metal, watching the clock, fingernails embedded in the steering wheel, and stress levels rising with every passing minute. The tractor that always lies in wait and pulls out in front of me just before North Cerney. The distended bladder caused by sucking agitatedly on my hydration pack as I sit in traffic in Bromsgrove. The back ache as I sink beneath the seat in order to hide my Wigan shirt as I pick my way through the Warrington traffic. Yes, I really should be glad of the rest.

But I'm a Wigan supporter. If you take away the rugby league season then you also take away my sense of purpose – my raison d'etre. So while it is true that the rugby season provides a series of hurdles that must be overcome, they are important hurdles. They might be tedious and tiring, but they also have the effect of enabling me to feel like I am making a contribution. I might not be putting in the big hits on the pitch, running my blood to water and scoring sensational tries for the team. But I am swearing at traffic on the motorway, and that means a lot to me.

People sometimes ask me what the rugby means to me. The answer I give them often surprises them. Watching my team win isn't as important to me as just watching my team. Oh, I've had my heart broken on numerous occasions within the confines of various stadia across the UK. And I've thrilled to the sensation of victory with the best of them. But on each occasion that my heart has been broken, I've been consoled by the fact that, no matter what the outcome, I have been watching the greatest game. It is about the event. It is about the skill and athleticism on the pitch. It is about the company – usually my father and a few close friends and familiar faces in the stands. It is about the camaraderie – not just with fellow supporters of my team but also with the opposition supporters and the neutrals. It is about the breaking down of barriers rather than the building of them. The shared experience, regardless of culture, creed and class. These are the foundations upon which our game was built. A proud past and an exciting future, to borrow a phrase. Our game has an ethos that enriches our lives, which is why we embrace its status as a family game, and why we jealously guard it (perhaps a little too jealously sometimes). As I sit in the empty wasteland between seasons, I can lean back, close my eyes and reflect on just how wonderful rugby league is. It is the distillation of the finest aspects of human nature.

Curse those off-season rose-tinted spectacles! Sometimes our game brings out the worst in us too. But mostly it brings out the best, and we need to cherish the best. Forget those negative voices who clamour against the seemingly protected status of such clubs as London and Les Catalans. Yes, let's protect our heartlands, but let's reach out at the same time. And judging by the way we interact as fans during our game's showcase finals, such a philosophy is not beyond us.

Sadly, throughout the off-season, such spiritually uplifting engagement eludes us at the very time we probably need it most. It leaves a dull, aching void in our lives. Even Christmas has been stripped of its most meaningful component – the annual Boxing Day showdown against St Helens. Without it, the festive period just isn't the same.

You know what Christmas is like – all the family converge on your house like a plague of grinning, elderly locusts. To your dismay, in the twinkling of a glass eye, your house turns into a retirement home. Relatives get dug up or sprung from secure units just so they can join you around the table. And then you all sit there, with your party hats on, grinning lifelessly at each other, having the same conversations you had last year. And all the time you're worrying about the number of sprouts that are being put away by the ones with the least amount of bodily control. Before long, you find yourself slumped in a vegetative state, breathing pure sprout gas and gazing through watering eyes at the blur of light that is your TV screen. Finally, once the Eastenders Christmas Special has robbed you of the will to live, you succumb to the lure of the family games.

You wake up the following morning face down in a jigsaw puzzle, with scrabble letters gummed to your cheeks and pockets full of Monopoly money. You need to get out. There is a world outside your window, and it's a world of activity and purpose. More importantly, it doesn't smell of recycled sprouts.

Our society reels listlessly through the Christmas period, none of us ever exactly certain of what day it is. Life without purpose is anathema to humans. We need something to rescue us from the Yuletide inertia – we need a jump-start for our flagging souls.

What fits the bill better than a full-blooded, death-or-glory rugby league clash of the titans? Nothing blows the cobwebs away quite like a good cathartic scream or two on the terraces while watching those big hits going in. It is what Boxing Day was made for. Besides, there was something special and heartening about turning out on Boxing Day. It felt vibrant, fresh and new. This was probably down to all those colourful new Christmas hats, coats and shiny St Helens shell-suits on display.

Summer rugby has robbed us not only of a traditional derby fixture but also of this much needed post-Christmas defibrillation.

So to return to my earlier question – am I glad of the rest provided to me by the winter off-season? The answer is a resounding "no". The rugby means too much to me. I will happily put up with all sorts of indignity and difficulty just to live in the radiant glow of our great game. And as much as I love to watch my team win, the real reason I am so sad in the off season is because rugby permeates my life with positivity and hope.

There is another negative aspect of the off-season that is rarely commented upon. As the weeks without rugby pass slowly by, we get out of the routine. While we remember the major, important things about the game, the enforced absence of matchday protocol creates the potential to forget certain aspects of rugby league etiquette. Those little rules and regulations that are rarely stated but generally acknowledged by everyone. On the first game back, you take your seat in the stadium with tiny nagging doubts that surface because your routines and patterns have been wiped from your memory during the long months of the off-season.

Little things like – when do we clap?

In many respects this is more than a tiny matter of etiquette. It is a deep philosophical question. Do we clap when the opposition team takes to the pitch? Do we clap when they score? For some these are agonising questions that re-surface at the start of a new season.

I've been a habitual clapper ever since I saw a bloody awful cabaret act in a Student Union bar. As I recall, it was a man whose singing was so bad that after each song he tried to re-engage the audience by performing increasingly desperate stunts. Finally, he was carried off after nearly choking himself while attempting to eat one of his own socks. There was a deathly silence, interrupted occasionally by the sound of a dismal singer regurgitating bits of fluff, as the stewards carrying him picked their way through the crowd. It was a terrible sight to behold. Suddenly, though, a friend of mine stood up and applauded for all he was worth. It was somehow infectious because minutes later the whole place was on its feet applauding, and the singer was visibly cheered. It was a curiously heart-warming moment. Later on I asked my friend why he did it. He told me that anybody who is prepared to perform for others deserves applause, no matter how good or bad they might be, just for giving it a go.

I liked this. Since then I have always clapped. I always clap the opposition team as they take to the pitch, no matter who they are. Without the opposition there would be no game. They deserve a clap just for that. Besides, it seems like good manners. One thing that has always struck me about rugby league is the gentlemanly conduct that pervades all aspects of the sport. There is little in the way of airs and graces, but instead there has always been a distinct feeling of "the right way to do things". It is an echo of the historical integrity of working class endeavour. Maybe much of that has been lost now, in our society of benefit-cheat-phobia and Jeremy Kyle confrontations. The traditional view of the honest, hard grafting working classes who retain their strong moral values in the face of terrible adversity has largely been replaced by that of the "chav". The media have embraced and championed this change of perspective, which in turn normalises it and turns it into something to aspire to. People might turn on me and say "don't talk wet, the idea of the 'honourable' working classes is just a myth." Yes, I understand that there has been some degree of romanticism afoot, and I am a realist at heart. But the fact remains that my grandparents had certain values. Whether it be never owning something until you have paid for it with hard earned money, or always clapping when the opposition team runs on – those values were noble, morally sound and they were decent. And they appear to be vanishing, judging from the number of people who prefer to boo opposition teams onto the pitch. Thankfully those wonderful old rugby league values are still evident when an opposition player is injured and has to be carried from the pitch. Everybody will stand up and clap them off. Moments like that make the hairs on the back of my neck stand on end. At other times, though, when I am being harangued for clapping as the opposition run on, or when they score a good try, I am overcome with sadness. Some people just don't seem to understand where our game has come from. Yet many of those same people like to harp on about respect, tradition and "the Wigan Way". If these things are so important then we should all be clapping the opposition, not just when they take to the pitch but also if they put together a decent bit of rugby. What are we afraid of? That it might be seen as disloyal? Or a weakness? No, it shows our strength. It shows that we are strong enough and big enough to behave properly. It is not disloyal. It puts others to shame.

There are other points of etiquette to remember as well. For instance, how many times is it acceptable to urinate during the course of a game? At what point does taking a pee become taking the pee? I have been blessed with a bladder that acts more like an unhindered tube. What goes in comes straight out. Furthermore, I do enjoy a few pints during a game. The upshot of this is that I just love those bits of music they play after tries and goals are scored. They are my Gents-Rush-Jingles. While everyone is still on their feet I squeeze past them and relieve my bladder. I've got it down to a fine art. As I'm leaping down the steps I'm already undoing the buttons on my flies. By the time I reach the troughs I am in the prone position. Three short blasts, rapid fire. Then I'm doing up my flies again one-handed as I'm running the tap with the other hand. Quick-swap-hands to ensure even coverage before I race back to my seat while fastening my flies back up with wet hands. The problem with this technique is that my crotch area is normally unsettlingly damp by the time I get there. Nobody has ever said anything, though, and let's face it, they shouldn't be looking. Furthermore, if they don't notice a wet crotch when it's waving about in their faces then I think it is safe to conclude that my toilet activity has not disrupted their enjoyment of the game to any serious degree.

The start of the new season is also the time to re-familiarise yourself with hat protocol. Personally, I'm not what you'd call a natural hat person. This is on account of the fact that hats just don't seem to like my head.

My head is shaped in such a way that the only thing that fits on with any degree of respectability is a paper bag. Hats, on the other hand, prefer to perch themselves on the highest point of my cranium in a constant struggle to disassociate themselves from the rest of me. The effect being that the hat always appears too small and my head too big. This happens regardless of the size of the hat and in spite of my repeated attempts to wedge it on, which makes my head a metaphysical phenomenon. It grows in relative proportion to the size of hats. Coming soon to a circus near you.

Hats at rugby matches used to be a simple, cut and dried affair. There was the flat cap (de rigueur for gentlemen of a certain age) and for the rest of us there was the "woolly bobbler." The flat cap has, in its favour, the benefit of tradition. It was what your granddad wore and his granddad before him and his granddad before him. And if it was good enough for them, then, by gum, it should be good enough for you. If you're a male over the age of eighteen then by now you have probably inherited one. It will be curling around the edges and is probably currently infusing your wardrobe with the unmistakeable odour of Brylcreem and old man. Not that this matters. It was passed down to you with the same awed reverence that is afforded the crown as it is bestowed upon the monarch. It is a rite of passage – a coming of age, handed down to you in your late teens on the understanding that you'll be wearing it with pride once it has festered in your wardrobe for another fifty years or so.

Down here in the south I have observed something of a resurgence of the flat cap among the youth of the home counties. They wear it, but they just don't *get* it. To them it is a folly, or a showy accessory worn at a rakish angle. I only ever saw my granddad wearing his flat cap at a rakish angle on one occasion. I suspect someone had spiked his mild.

The flat cap is a badge of honour among the older generations of the working classes. That's where it belongs and that's where it should stay. You know this to be true. It is the reason why whenever you see a toff in a flat cap you have that inexplicably overwhelming urge to punch him in the face.

For these reasons flat caps are entirely acceptable attire at rugby league games for those who have first-hand recollection of the 1950s.

As for the woolly bobbler, there lies a far sadder tale. The bobble hat is all but extinct. The days when cherry and white striped bobble hats were synonymous with rugby league games disappeared with the dawn of summer rugby. It used to be a necessary inclusion in your match-day kit list, but alas, is no more. The thing is, everybody looks universally silly in bobble hats. When it's cold and the need to insulate your head is of paramount importance then you simply cannot underestimate the effectiveness of what is essentially a woolly tea cosy. If they're good enough for your tea pot then they're surely good enough for your head. In fact I think I once even wore an actual tea cosy to a rugby match. It was warm and would have made the perfect balaclava for a Cyclops. I'd never get away with wearing it to a match now, though. Summer rugby has stripped away our final refuge from self-consciousness. When it's cold and warmth takes priority over appearance, we'll stick anything on our heads. Warmer climates enable us to choose our attire out of taste rather than necessity. If it wasn't for heat we would never hear "does my bum look big in this?" One of the overlooked side effects of global warming is that I expect we'll hear a lot more of that sort of thing. Not that you'd wear a bobble hat on your bum, I'm not saying that. Although a tea cosy, if adequately stretched, would make a nice warm pair of underpants that wouldn't even have to be removed during toilet visits. This would possibly save extra precious seconds during the Gents-Rush-Jingles.

These days the rugby hat options are somewhat depleted and, for those too young for flat caps and not enamoured with baseball caps, there is only the novelty hat left as viable headwear. In essence this means either the "hilariously" tall top hats made from the sort of fabric you associate with house fires, or the comedic jester's hat. Jesters were never funny. This is a historical fact. The only thing that the ruling classes ever found remotely amusing about jesters was having them put to death. Their hats were even less funny. If ever a hat cried out "execute me!"

it was the jester's hat. They are the headwear equivalent of the novelty tie. Admit it, your impulse upon seeing a man in a novelty tie is exactly the same as when you see a toff in a flat cap. A man who is wearing a novelty tie is trying too hard to advertise his sense of humour. This is because he doesn't have one. He doesn't have a girlfriend either. He probably does have a jester's hat, though, and he wears it to the rugby.

Such sociological implications of the hat ("hatology", if you will) are negligible, however, when compared to the practical issues of wearing hats to rugby games. Flat caps are perfect – they are designed specifically so that you can see right over the top of them. A man sat in front of you in a flat cap will give you no bother at all. Someone sat in front of you in a bobble hat might potentially unleash your inner cat but will otherwise have a minimal impact on your enjoyment of the game. An elongated, highly flammable top hat, on the other hand, will inevitably impede your view and, if you're in the habit of having a crafty fag when the stewards' backs are turned, might just cause a small-scale re-enactment of The Towering Inferno. Whereas jesters' hats will definitely have your eye out every time a try is scored.

Then there are flags. Like hats, flags at rugby matches do look like a lot of fun. It is hard to think of anybody waving a flag and not having fun because flags are intrinsically happy things. How could a colourful bit of cloth on a stick be anything but happy? Unless it is being waved in defiance, or intimidation, or when it has been planted in your back yard by an occupying foreign force. Other than that, I'd say they're pretty cheerful. They brighten up the place no end. As much as I have come to love the DW Stadium, it has to be said that concrete-chic doesn't provide the most engaging of colour schemes. Regardless of what the middle aged women at work tell you, there is a limit to the amount of fun you can have with fifty shades of grey. That's why it is nice to have a few colourful flags and banners flapping from the rafters and waving in the stands. All it takes is a bit of flapping and waving to generate a real party atmosphere at even the most insignificant fixture on the list. It is what your soul has been crying out for during those long, dark, grim off-season weekends. Not just the flags, but the other paraphernalia – big foam pointy hands, cards that say "TRY" and NO TRY" on alternate sides, hooters, honkers and vuvuzelas. They all contribute to the festival of fun that is a Wigan Warriors rugby game. This all appeals greatly to me because I'm the sort of person who wears a Hawaiian shirt on holiday.

The same can't be said of all spectators, though. A number of my fellows over on the West are less appreciative of this sort of thing. The bloke who sits in front of me, for instance, does not like me clapping too loudly. It hurts his ears. He's a lovely chap and at the start of every season I am genuinely pleased to see him. But I have a feeling that if I blew on a vuvuzela in his immediate vicinity, his head would pop. Similarly, the couple behind me get unsettled when I momentarily obscure their view during the Gents

Rush Jingles. If I was to spend half the game waving a flag in their faces they might find it necessary to murder me. And there's a woman down my row who gives me a filthy look whenever I get my honker out. She's not the first to turn her nose up at my honker and she won't be the last.

As I have previously noted, this is not a slur on the characters of these individuals, nor is it any kind of complaint. It is merely an observation of the fact that different sections of the community have different customs and social norms. It is a form of microcosmic cultural diversity and you need to be aware of it before you strike up your one-man-band in the wrong stand. The flags and hooters make for a wonderful, exciting spectacle, particularly on TV where we might pick up impressionable new young supporters – the ones who say "Lol" and "YOLO" a lot and can't enjoy themselves unless they have a flag to wave – as a result.

Fortunately these doubts are negated by the welcome return of not just the game itself, but of all the other wonderful little things about watching rugby. The little fixes that help build the whole experience. Golden Gambling, for instance. How I always loved to see the wonderful and dearly missed Gordon "Golden Gamble" Harrison striding onto the pitch in his golden suit. A touch of class by anybody's standards (surely?). There aren't many men who can carry off a gleaming suit of gold and a top hat. Many visiting spectators might have scoffed at the sight of him, and while I still maintain that gold-coloured clothing is almost exclusively for post-menopausal women, Gordon always seemed to look just right. Somehow he never failed to take me by surprise at the start of a season. I would always have a little moment of shock as he appeared, strolling onto the pitch like a bar of human bullion. But I loved it! I'd raise my plastic glass of beer to him and feel safe and secure in the knowledge that the world was back on track. And then I'd sit back and enjoy the inertia of the half-time interval and whatever display of entertainment had been provided to bide the time before the second half.

These days it is the "Warrior Girls." Like Gordon's suit, they may not be to everybody's taste, but, nonetheless, they are now an integral part of the match-day experience. They say watching a game at home on TV doesn't come close to actually sampling that experience in real life. I put this largely down to the fact that there are not nearly enough high-kicking legs in sparkly brown tights parading through my living room during the advert break. I have, naturally, pleaded with Mrs Macaulay to do what she can to remedy this (I even bought her the tights) but her response wasn't altogether encouraging. For once she found herself in agreement with my father.

He doesn't like the dancing girls either. It is all too much like what he calls a "Pagan Fertility Ritual" for his tastes. This is fair enough. Some men want nubile, jiggling, high-kicking Pagan virgins, while others are happy with the Pemberton District Brass Band. Playing the Floral Dance.

One thing that the half-time dancing phenomenon does do, is it provides a large female contingent with an active and valued role in the match-day proceedings. Anything that encourages more people into rugby league at whatever level or capacity has got to be positive. Or maybe I've just persuaded myself to believe that, because the alternative would be to admit that I've got a thing for sparkly tights. I pine for them during the off-season.

One of the really harsh aspects of our off-season is that it seems to be at the time when all other sports are right in the full pomp of their on-season. It is almost as if they're deliberately rubbing it in. They are looking down their noses at us as they revel in the mud and the rain and the bone-bending cold of the British winter.

There are some definite advantages to watching rugby in winter. For one thing, it gives you an opportunity to get out of the house. If, like me, you're the sort of person who peeps out through the curtains and, upon seeing the cold, driving rain, crawls back under the duvet, then the pressing matter of a rugby game would be just the incentive to get out into the fresh air. Unless the rugby game is in Widnes, in which case the air under your duvet is probably fresher.

And, of course, by the same token, if you're out of your house then there is the social aspect. Too many people spend the winter months boxed in and cut off from society. They sit indoors, devoid of the stimulation of social interaction. At least when you're at the rugby you are mingling with thousands of people and engaging in social intercourse and stimulating debate. Unless the rugby game is in Hull, in which case there is probably more stimulation to be found under your duvet.

Here I suppose I am being a little unfair. Having lived in Hull for a whole year, I should know better than to suggest that people in Hull are not stimulating company. For the record, this is definitely not the case. What I did find was that the people of Hull were overwhelmingly effusive – but only once they'd got the measure of you. Until then you were just an outsider. But once you'd proved yourself, they would clasp you to their bosom. And I've been clasped to a fair few bosoms in Hull. It is very warming. It is also probably the best way to ward off the biting east coast chill. You've not really, truly felt the cold until you've experienced the full onslaught of winter in Hull. Another reason to support winter rugby is that if people in Hull can cope with turning out for rugby matches in the dead of winter, then the rest of us really have no excuse. Winter in Wigan looks like a Caribbean holiday when you're from Hull.

We have all at some point had to cope with being far too cold for comfort. Hypothermia is not a particularly nice thing. If I'm going to go hypothermic anywhere, though, I think I'd like it to be at a rugby ground. I'd especially like it to be at the DW Stadium. It would be the closest I'd ever come to "turning blue" in Wigan. As the cold creeps in, freezing my extremities and playing havoc with my core body temperature, at least I'd have the satisfaction of knowing that even in my hour of direst need I didn't succumb to the temptation of a warming cup of rugby league ground hot Bovril. Such a feat in itself would be a triumph worthy of the ending of my life. As they lowered me into my grave (I'm guessing I'd still be too frozen for a cremation – unless they microwaved me first) the assembled mourners would take off their flat caps and say "You know, he was only ten feet away from the lifesaving warmth of a cup of hot Bovril. But he was a man of principle!"

The principle being that I will never again allow anything that tastes like the urine of a diabetic hound reared on a diet of beef cup-a-soups to pass my lips.

I'm not saying that Bovril itself is at fault. Indeed, there have been occasions when I have quite enjoyed a cup of steaming hot Bovril. Nor would I wish to suggest that the Bovril served up at the DW Stadium is in any way substandard.

It's just that I will never forget my first ever encounter with hot Bovril at a rugby league ground. It was Central Park, back in the post-relegation upheaval period of the mid 1980s. A typically dark, cold and wet winter's Sunday afternoon when my enjoyment of the game was being ruined by my incessant shaking and the sound of my rattling teeth. My father decided that this was the moment for my first rugby league Bovril experience. And he was probably guilty of building up my hopes a little too much.

"It's wonderful stuff."

"It will warm you up a treat."

"With this inside you, you won't feel the cold at all."

At least that last statement was true. I was so busy retching that I completely forgot about the cold.

Back in those days it seemed there was some dark art to the preparation of Bovril at rugby league grounds. An art that made it taste like the devil's own ear wax (with added beef flavouring).

I'm sure that the Foods Standards Agency has since ensured that such satanic methodology in the preparation of Bovril is a thing of the past. I'm sure Bovril at the DW Stadium now tastes absolutely divine. Nevertheless, memories run deep and it will be an exceptionally cold day in hell[17] before I buy a cup of the stuff again. One of the marvellous things about summer rugby is that it minimises moments of Bovril temptation.

Are there any other reasons why we might consider a return to winter rugby? You could build a case around the apparent increased frequency of injuries since the advent of the summer era. You could argue that sun-baked, firmer pitches are responsible for these injuries. Ankles, knees, hips, backs, shoulders and arms are less cushioned on the hard, dry grounds and are subject to collisions of far greater force due to the extra speed afforded on these hard pitches. The repeated poundings and impacts are taking their toll on our players' joints and bones.

But then again you might just as well suggest that full time professionalism, improved training regimes and

17   Or Hull.

a more evenly matched competition have had the effect of raising standards and creating a far more physically demanding sport. Hence the injuries. Besides, running ankle-deep in mud, attempting to change direction at speed on soggy surfaces and moving from the cosy warmth of the changing room to bone-jarring tackles in sub-zero temperatures are all high-risk activities, injury-wise. In fact, dehydration, heat stroke and sun burn provide a much stronger argument against summer rugby on health grounds. And not just for the players, but for the supporters too. As a nation we tend to underestimate the dangers associated with hot weather. We're notorious for it. Only mad dogs and Englishmen venture out in the midday sun. But, in defence of mad dogs, they're mad. Whereas we perfectly sane Brits will tear off our clothes and launch ourselves, dripping in oil, into the open at the first tentative glimpse of the sun peeping through the clouds.

To keep a sense of perspective, the players are our club's most valuable commodity, and they are well protected. Sun lotion, rapid-rehydration drinks, more substitutions, more players on the bench and the option of playing in quarters rather than halves are steps the sport can and does take to reduce the risk of serious harm.

Another argument I have heard against summer rugby is the notion that summer is a time for family holidays. By staging games during the summer holiday period you are either denying holidaying fans the opportunity to watch their team (which is especially galling if they are season ticket holders who have already paid for the game) or denying really dedicated supporters the chance to go on holiday.

Notwithstanding the opposition I get from my wife in my endeavours to attend more games, I have to dismiss this argument as a non-starter. If, like me, you live over one hundred miles away from the DW Stadium, and you're a teacher who can't work flexible hours, then the six week summer holiday is the ideal time to watch rugby games. You can see as many as six of them on the bounce if you're really lucky. It's not that I don't get to see the games during term time, but the hassle of the post 5pm motorway network makes it a testing experience. When there is no school I can set off early. I can take my children to stay with grandma and relieve the pressure on my long-suffering wife who can, in turn, go shopping with all the money we don't have. Everyone's a winner!

It is important that we don't forget that while followers of other sports are enduring the highs and lows, ebbs and flows and swings and roundabouts of outrageous sporting fortune during their regular season, we rugby league devotees lie in a state of grace. It is that timeless span between the final whistle of the previous season and the first whistle of the next season. In spite of all its drawbacks and inert deadness, this is a wonderful time to be a fan. These are the dark winter days of endless dreams. A time when you can let the disappointments and angst of the last season drift away. Release those negative thoughts – let them go free! And in their place welcome in the burning hope of optimism. You've earned it.

Finally, the day will come when the new season begins, and what a day that is! It is hard to explain how it feels. I mean, it feels good, obviously, but there are various levels and shades of good. Some gooder than others. The dawn of a new season, though, is right up there with the goodest of them. It is on a par with the moment I first discovered what happens to vodka when you put jelly babies in it. No, actually it's better than that. It's as good as the moment I first discovered what happens to jelly babies when you put them in vodka. That sums it up far more accurately. The reason that the jelly baby/vodka discovery was so special, I think, was that it essentially encapsulated the fusion of the multi-coloured joy of youth together with the excitement of intoxication. And it tasted of jelly babies.

This is of note because in so many ways the upcoming season will be exactly like a bag of jelly babies. There will be such a colourful assortment of experiences to be enjoyed. The black ones you absolutely love and experience with a sense of total and utter joy – convincing victories over teams like Saints, Wire and Leeds. Then there are the red ones. Fun away days to places like London, Wales, France and Barrow. There are the orange ones – those games Wigan win convincingly against teams that you know full well that Wigan should beat easily. Then there are the yellow games where we win against lesser teams, but not especially convincingly. You feel a bit yellow as you walk away, and the win is something of a relief. As for the green games, we don't talk about them.

Of course, you know that you are desperately ready for the beginning of the new season when you get so anxious that you start to compare rugby league games to a bag of jelly babies. As for the vodka, well, I enjoy a few drinks prior to each match. It calms my nerves.

So how, exactly should we open our bag of jelly babies? In what way should the exciting, vibrant new Super League season announce its birth?

In 2011 the RFL saw fit to open the season with a fanfare – a big "We're Back!" event to mark the end of the winter and the beginning of the new Super league season. Basically, they moved the "Magic" event from sunny May to shivery February.

This was actually the first Magic weekend that I attended. Prior to this I had been a somewhat bemused bystander, watching from my sofa with a curious mixture of envy and confusion. All those supporters seemed to be having a whale of a time, and I wanted to be part of that. But for the life of me I couldn't figure out where all the fun was coming from. It seemed to be a cup final atmosphere without the cup final. Somehow it felt false to me. Like some genetically engineered hybrid beast cobbled together by a mad scientist. Or some elaborate social experiment to ascertain the psychological effects of long trips and big stadia on rugby league fans. The result: sporadic outbursts of fancy dress, heavy drinking and the flagrant (and fragrant) acquisition of countless little bottles of Travelodge shampoo-cum-bubble bath. And all for what? No trophy, hub-cap or shield. Just another two points in the league table. Two points that, important as they might be, are still no more or less important than any other two points you might pick up or lose during the course of the season. It is the equivalent of turning up at a relative's house on a random day of the year and insisting that they celebrate their birthday there and then. And invite the rest of the family round too. Make them stay in a Travelodge and wear fancy dress. And force feed your granny three whole bottles of advocaat (she can take it – grannies can always find room for alcoholic custard). Then go home and pretend the whole thing never happened. Your granny won't remember anyway. Now that's what I call "Magic."

But there I was, finally, having made the effort to travel to Cardiff, enjoying the bizarre atmosphere along with everybody else. Admittedly, I really couldn't claim to have made a particularly massive effort to get there. For me it was far easier than a trip to a match at the DW Stadium.

I did enjoy the event, I have to admit. The excitement of a new Super League season managed to blend seamlessly with that wonderful feeling you get when rugby league followers invade a neutral town. This generated a very special atmosphere. A few beers in Cardiff's excellent city centre bars and pubs helped as well. In many ways it felt like a great success. But then there was the game.

It doesn't sound too bad on the face of it – a hard fought draw against St Helens with a few good tries and some crunching defence. Except there was something not quite right about it. This was, after all, the season's first game and it had the feel of a pre-season friendly. The neutral location and the vast stadium served to divorce the game from the reality of the regular season, which didn't help, especially at such an early stage. Mostly, though, the problem lay with the fact that neither side was ready for an epic clash. The off-season rustiness was only too evident.

Starting the season with the Magic event turned out to be a short-lived experiment in the end. In my view this was a bit of a pity. While I take the point that you don't really want a major showcase event at a time when your new key players haven't quite figured out how to pass to each other yet, I still think it is a wonderful idea to start the season with a real bang. That's what we need – an explosion of jelly baby colour and excitement in deepest, darkest February. Every Super League season should start with us grabbing the world by its lapels and giving it a good shake. A bit of a fanfare to let them know we've arrived. The sleep is over. The darkness dissipates and the freeze thaws. We've been away for a little while, lying dormant, resting and recharging. But with the end of winter and just before the earliest sign of spring, we will explode into life. Rugby league is back!

WIGAN WORRIERS

As the 2012 season drew to a close with the Warriors cementing their place at the top of the table, having treated us to a campaign of thrilling rugby, I thought we were having a good time. I really did. We had been dancing on the terraces and singing in the stands. We had beaten St Helens again, and again, and again. We had dismantled the Rhinos and then murdered them just to make sure. And at the very end of the regular season, the Wigan Warriors lifted the League Leaders Shield and we were all jubilant.

Or so I thought.

Just a few short weeks later I was scrolling through the internet forums expecting to be engaged in the usual off-season optimistic banter. But it wasn't there. In its place there lay a cloud of utter despair. The woe was hanging heavy in the air and curling the corners of my computer screen. For the life of me I couldn't understand why this was the case. Yes, we had failed to reach a final during that season, and yes, we had just been knocked out of the game's most meaningful competition by Leeds. Again. But this had happened in a scintillating game of rugby league that could quite literally have gone either way and was lost due to an interception try and an exceptional kicker. It was a disappointing outcome, riddled with anguish, but hardly the cause for the sort of doomy and gloomy despondency that was playing havoc with my pixels.

It occurred to me at the time that we can be guilty of wallowing in negativity sometimes. This is putting it mildly. In fact the reality is that, as a body of supporters, we have a tendency to embrace despair at the drop of a flat (salary) cap.

There are several reasons why this might be the case. Many of them are largely due to human nature and the way that we react as a species to the stimulation provided by the sport we love.

While words like "stimulation" and "love" are popping up, let's talk about sex. For instance, I can reveal that I'm not into group sex. Sex, for me, is not a group activity. This is mainly because finding more than one person willing to have sex with me at any one time is something of a logistical nightmare. Actually, when I think about it, finding just one person willing to have sex with me at all is something of a logistical nightmare. This is despite the fact that I am happily married. When it comes to the "whether or not to have sex with me" equation, my wife has all the reservations of a complete stranger with the added downside that she knows me well enough to know better.

This is a pity. Because, by virtue of our genetically hardwired instincts for survival and self-replication, sex happens to be one of the most enjoyable experiences known to mankind. There is surely nothing better.

Unless, that is, you were lucky enough to be present at Wembley Stadium during the 1994 Challenge Cup final when Martin Offiah scored THAT try against Leeds.

I'll never forget it. Pressure against us, close to our own line. Some crunching defence by an invigorated Leeds side, followed by a slack play the ball and a fairly innocuous pass out from Gary Connelly. (This is all foreplay). Then the ball is picked up by "Chariots" in a position where there is seemingly nothing doing; and yet ...suddenly... inexplicably...a break – a palpable break! Offiah scoots past the would-be tacklers and then he hits the accelerator, hard. The Leeds players desperately try to form a rear-guard defensive action, which fails. Offiah is away and clear, his legs pumping as he turns Alan Tait inside-out on his way to the corner. The whole stadium is on its feet, the roar is deafening – a wall of sound made up of several thousand voices, all of them screaming with ferocious urgency. Individual words and voices are lost in this cacophonous explosion (apart from three clear words emanating from somewhere to my left – "OPEN...YOUR...LEGS!"). And as Martin Offiah touched that ball down, amidst the fury and the elation and the complete madness of the moment I turned to my father and screamed the sort of expletive that would have shocked my current West Stand compatriots to the core. It was a bad word. But, strangely, it was actually a good word to use at the time because that moment seemed almost orgasmic. And bearing in mind the size of the crowd it remains the closest that I have ever come to having group sex in my life.

And it was wonderful. I make no apologies for the sexual analogy because moments like that are as raw and as passionate as any sexual encounter can be and they carry with them the same depth of emotion. Actually, I'd probably go as far as to say that that moment was better than sex.

Maybe I've just not been having sex with the right people. Interestingly, though, I have a very vivid recollection of walking away from Wembley Stadium that afternoon and feeling…miserable. It wasn't because of the outcome of the game. It wasn't because of anything at all, really. It was probably just because I had been emotionally catapulted to the highest possible zenith of elation and at some point I had to make the descent back to reality.

It makes me wonder whether the willingness of Wigan supporters to embrace despair and despondency at the end of a largely successful season is the rugby league equivalent of a post-coital comedown.

Or maybe it is even simpler than that. Maybe it is merely the other side of the emotional coin. We glean so much pleasure and enjoyment from watching Wigan that it has to be balanced by a strong dose of dismay. This would suggest some sort of bi-polar relationship with the sport and is perhaps indicative of the human need to go through both highs and lows in order to fully appreciate an experience.

As George Bernard Shaw once said;

"A lifetime of happiness! No man alive could bear it: it would be hell on earth."

This implies that a certain amount of suffering is essential to our wellbeing. And also to our enjoyment of the game. We are creatures capable of feeling emotions right across the spectrum and therefore we cannot truly enjoy something unless it gives us access to the full gamut of emotional response. This would certainly explain our eagerness to embrace desolation so readily.

Or maybe it's because we're just miserable bastards, who knows? In any case, we cannot avoid the truth of the matter. We can be incredibly negative and pessimistic in our outlook even at times when you'd think we should be quite happy. We really are the Wigan Worriers. In an attempt to both acknowledge and explore this assertion, what follows is a list of the things that, in the main, we are worried about.

WORRY NUMBER ONE :THE SIGNING OF QUALITY PLAYERS.

One of the most predictable and obvious forms of angst is generated by the club's activities (or lack thereof) in the transfer market. Wigan fans demand star players. We've been brought up on a diet of star players. In fact sometimes it feels like it's the only diet we've ever had. And it has certainly been a rich diet. We have variously chomped happily on Boiled Edwards, Farrell Fritters, Terrine of Tomkins, Charnley Chops, Cajun Clarke, Betts Burgers, Rack of Robinson, Radlinski Rarebit and Hashed Hock.

And that's just the tip of the iceberg lettuce. After such immensely pleasurable culinary delights, the signing of players perceived to be of a more average hue can feel like walking out of the Savoy and heading for the Little Chef. It is, therefore, hardly surprising that the cherry and white scarved Egon Ronays of the DW stands insist on the signing of players of the highest quality prior to the start of each new season. It isn't a request. It isn't even a demand. It's an expectation. It goes hand in hand with the expectation that every season should bring success and beautiful, gleaming trophies. In fact we don't just want beautiful, gleaming trophies. We want trophies delivered by the most beautiful, gleaming players in the game. It is what we deserve, for we are Wigan. And within this line of thought there is the clear correlation between the signing of marquee players (more often than not from overseas) and success. This is an entirely valid and logical line of thought. You cannot hope to argue against the notion that signing excellent players will make for an excellent team with an excellent chance of success. You know it makes sense. Logic dictates that a Wigan chairman who does not sign at least a couple of star players every year is not doing his job properly.

The problem is, it's never really as clear cut as that. Look back at the menu of exceptional Wigan players I provided earlier. It won't have escaped your notice that it was a menu of organic, home-grown fayre. Some of those players admittedly came from beyond the borders of Wigan Parish Council, and many of them have gone a lot further since. Nonetheless, they all came up through the ranks of the youth system prior to making it big in the first team. And there have been many others who have come through that self-same system and gone on to become established stars in other Super League teams, NRL sides and Union clubs. The evidence would seem to suggest that we have a very good youth system at Wigan. We breed excellent players who rise through the ranks together, having developed an understanding of each other and, you would hope, have a real sense of commitment and belonging to the club. In my own view this is where our future lies. Recruitment should be targeted at youngsters who will arrive with their youthful blend of zest, enthusiasm, impudence and eagerness to conquer all. I would say this, of course. I'm an educationalist, and as such I happen to think a lot of our country's youth. Moreover, I like the idea that in times of recession a community rugby club will take on youngsters who may or may not have been able to hold their heads above water academically. There is currently a dearth of institutions that are prepared to support such youngsters. I'd like to think that a club like Wigan would embrace those with a flair for the sport, or even those who are just prepared to slog their guts out for it. To nurture them, enhance them, provide them with opportunities and a further education. And to turn as many of them as possible into crowd-pleasing superstars of the future. Wherever they ended up plying their rugby trade, I would still consider it a job well done. That is my dream. It is, perhaps, a lonely and oft-dismissed dream in the dog-eat-dog world of competitive professional sport, but I hold it dear.

Mind you, when I'm on my feet in the West Stand looking on in despair as a team full of expensive imports and poached prima donnas breaks our defensive line, then I'm with the rest of them. Let's buy some superstars! Short term heartache is a bit of a bugger, isn't it? I mean, what we all want is success and winning and for everything to be shiny. All the time. Long term security and achievement is in the purview of the administrators. We fans can afford to lose ourselves in our lust for instant gratification, good rugby, trophies and hot pies.

We should take the time to remember that it hasn't always entirely been Egon Ronay or Savoy standard at Wigan. Nothing says "chicken-in-a-basket" louder than the mention of Doc Murray. You don't get more "Findus Crispy Pancake" than Shem Tatupu. And on numerous occasions I have accidentally ordered Paul Koloi instead of Spam. It's an easy mistake to make. I'm not saying there is anything remotely wrong with chicken in a basket, Findus Crispy Pancakes or Spam. There isn't. I myself can wholeheartedly recommend such fodder as a cheap and endurable alternative to…um…nicer food. But whatever you do, don't serve them to your betrothed on Valentine's Day. I would suggest that they are not quite the right gastronomic option for a romantic candlelit dinner for two. Just as the aforementioned players were not quite the right ingredients to add fuel to our passionate romance with the rugby. And even if you do choose to serve such meals up to your girlfriend on Valentine's Day, don't announce them with a tremendous fanfare as "the next Tuigamala". Her love for you might just overcome a multitude of shortcomings, but it's going to be seriously tested by that sort of beef extract.

I appreciate that I have just run the risk of upsetting three men who I know practically nothing about. That was not my intention. For all I know, Doc Murray, Shem Tatupu and Paul Koloi might be the nicest individuals anybody could hope to meet. Furthermore they have done nothing wrong. They were given the opportunity to play for one of the world's leading rugby league teams and they grabbed that opportunity with both hands (apart from Doc Murray who fumbled it just in front of his own try line). You can't blame them for that. There is no wrongdoing. They were ambitious and they did what any one of us would have done had we been offered a chance like that. The problem isn't even that they were offered a chance like that in the first place. The problem is that they were signed not as long term projects, but as the answer to the loss of some of our established star players. They may well have had tremendous potential, but that potential was extinguished by the club's desperation. Who knows, in another era, under a different management system, those players might well have scaled the heights. In the event it felt like false promises, desperation and cynicism. It didn't feel like Wigan.

In all fairness the answers probably lie somewhere between the two philosophies. Success will not be achieved by a good youth system alone – at some point every club with ambition will have to splash the cash on a bit of flash. The purchasing of rugby league players is of course a fine art in itself and sometimes it works perfectly. The right buy at the right time can herald a whole new optimistic era for a club. I remember how it felt when we signed players like Henderson Gill and Graeme West. Back then it didn't feel like we simply had to buy great players just because they were great players. They felt like strategic buys. They were a statement of intent, a tactical advantage, a shot in the arm and a splash of colour. Somewhere along the line all that changed and the star players became an expectation, or even worse – an entitlement. But then other teams were snapping at our heels and buying star players of their own. The difference, I think, was that we had our secret weapon – the solid backbone that was our youth conveyor belt. People might scoff and say (in thickest Yorkshire) "Nay lad, it were because Wigan were full time professionals". They are just wide of the mark. Full time professionalism was what afforded us the advantage of having such an excellent youth system. That was what made the difference.

People will always look back on those heady days of seemingly unlimited budgets and mega-signings and associate them with the club's unparalleled successes. The association is only too clear in the minds of those who call for the club to spend every penny right up to the very limit of the salary cap. Their mantra is "Spend! Spend! Spend!" on the assumption that paying bigger wages is the key to success. This is in spite of an economic climate that has seen a succession of sporting clubs and countless other business empires crumble before our eyes. The spend-the-lot proponents rationalise their position with trite statements along the lines of "well, you see, running a rugby league club is different to running any other sort of business – you have to expect it to run at a loss." I would love to be a fly on the wall watching that particular conversation with the bank manager. In fact I might even try it when I am next summoned into my own local branch. I will look my Personal Banker right in the eye and say "Well, you see, running me is different to running any other sort of bank customer. I'm expected to have a huge overdraft. Because I'm me. You have to run me at a loss."

[EXIT, PURSUED BY A BANK MANAGER].

There is undeniably *some* truth in this line of argument. I am definitely useless with money – that is certainly true. Should I ever be fortunate enough to acquire a sugar daddy then he would find me to be extremely high maintenance. But there is no reason or excuse for it. And there's no reason why I shouldn't have to work harder to provide greater value for a smaller investment. I can't accept that it shouldn't be the same for rugby clubs. We currently have two competitions in our domestic game, providing three separate trophies – namely the Challenge Cup, the League Leader's Shield and the Super League Trophy. We now have twelve teams all competing for these three trophies. Clearly they can't all get one. You would need twelve different trophies for that to be the case, and possibly more because sneaky teams like Leeds would probably try to win more than one. If this happened then our domestic competition would be rendered as meaningless as a game of pass the parcel at a four year old's birthday party. I've hosted such a party – every child has to win exactly the same bag of sweets that every other child wins. In my view it robs the game of the most entertaining bit – watching the losers' tantrums.

You can't turn rugby league into a non-competitive party game. Nobody wants that. Those who insist it is each team's duty to spend the full amount of the salary cap on players' wages are conveniently forgetting that at least nine teams will not win a trophy. In other words, if you adopt the mantra that your club has to spend to the limit of the cap, you are paying for an seventy five per cent chance of failure. This is crazy. You can actually achieve failure a lot cheaper than £1.7 million. I manage it every year on a meagre teacher's salary. This puts the demands of those fans into perspective. What they are basically saying is "I don't mind us not winning anything providing I know we've spent as much as we can on not winning anything."

Even more worrying are those people who cry out for the salary cap to be scrapped altogether. They say it shows a "lack of ambition" on the part of the sport.

This sticks in my throat. A "lack of ambition" on the part of rugby league – one of the most innovative and forward-thinking sports our country boasts? Can we seriously dismiss a sensible and realistic limit on club spending as a lack of ambition? It is a mechanism that will potentially prevent those few teams with wealthy backers from monopolising the competition. The fact that Wigan currently happens to be in the fortunate position of having just such a backer shouldn't make us a nailed-on, dead certainty for a trophy. I don't want to see rugby league becoming a sport of lucrative sheep clubs looking down their noses at skinflint goat clubs. There's too much of that going on in our country as it is. I want clubs to be financially successful because they attract viewers, fans, sponsorship and satellite businesses. I want them to achieve this by being good clubs rather than by dint of being the over-privileged play things of wealthy businessmen. I don't want my rugby league club to be the sporting equivalent of a trophy wife – all leopard skin, glitter, manicure and make-up but not much going on behind the façade. A rugby league club shouldn't be a director's box on legs, it should be better than that. Is that not an ambitious enough goal for some people?

For what it's worth, I think that the salary cap is a good idea as long as it is set and maintained at a level that all clubs could potentially afford given capacity crowds and some acknowledgement of other peripheral income and revenue streams that each and every Super League club should be encouraged to cultivate. Now that is definitely ambitious. Going a step further, would it not also be a sign of an ambitious club to *not* feel obliged to spend every penny of the cap?

I understand the view that better players demand higher wages and that they will only agree to play for a club if they are ensured their highest possible income. It is the assumption that people on assured high salaries will always perform better than those on lower salaries. This would be fine if it happened to be generally true of human beings. It isn't though, is it? The lessons learned from the cases of the Lehman Brothers, Fred "The Shred" Goodwin and countless others would seem to tell us that life simply doesn't work like that.

A combination of enticing salaries and further incentives to be awarded on the basis of successful performance seems to make far more sense. If I was a multi-millionaire owner of a Super League club that's the basis I would use for setting players wages. I would do this in the hope that it might:

a. bring about success and
b. stop people thinking that my club is some sort of tarty trophy wife.

WORRY NUMBER TWO: REFEREES.

Just in case she happens to be reading this, I would like to take this opportunity to state, quite categorically, that my wife is most definitely not some sort of tarty trophy wife.

She is nothing of the sort, and our relationship

couldn't be further removed from that of a sugar daddy and a painted strumpet. Sadly.

No, we have a very different sort of relationship. She calls the shots. And then she shoots me. When she says "Jump!", I say, "how high?" Having agreed on the height of the jump, I am somehow expected to add a few unspoken extra inches. Then, when I inevitably fall short, I am penalised.

In fact you could say that our relationship is more akin to that between a referee and a player. And I have a propensity for being offside.

This worries us both greatly, which isn't at all surprising because, like me, most Wigan fans also seem to be greatly worried about the referee. Here we are not alone, for what rugby league follower doesn't worry about the referee? Personally, at the very mention of the word "referee" I am regressed to a time before I even met my wife, to an afternoon sat in a sixth form classroom taking down the following dictated notes:

"Have you recently enjoyed a decent game of soccer, rugby or tennis? If the answer is 'yes', then it is probably because you had a good referee…"

Quite frankly I am amazed that I can still remember those words. They were the opening lines of my very first Politics lesson. Even as I sat there, furiously scribbling away in my rather unfortunate left-handed style, I was thinking "this is total bobbins!" Neither my hand nor my mind were able to keep pace with Doctor Jones' dictated notes. My hand rebelled and started doodling quite exhilarating depictions of a journey into the inner psyche of a lava lamp while my mind conjured up replays of some of Wigan's most recent matches. In those mental re-runs, there was no evidence of any referee. I had subliminally edited him out. This, I noted, made no difference to my enjoyment of the reminiscences. I was then able to conclude that

a. I had taken inaccurate notes.
b. My teacher was weird.
c. He probably hadn't seen many decent games of soccer, rugby or tennis.

My conclusions were incorrect. The referee is a vital part of any game, and I think we all know this. Yet, regardless of the fact that without him there could be no game, we all love to hate the referee[18]. Even the most liberal-minded do-gooders among us (and I'm probably talking about me when I say that) tend to harbour a grudge towards the merry whistle blowing man in the middle. We just can't help ourselves, and the reason why is simple. He is the law[19]. He represents authority. When things don't go our way we find it necessary to point accusing fingers at authority and outline its ineptitude. We do this, of course, because we like to think that we know better.

---

18   This is not the case with my wife.

19   This is the case with my wife.

This is why refereeing is a thankless job. You have to admire the sort of person who goes to work knowing that their day will end with a few thousand people angrily jeering and gesticulating at them. And that's on a good day. On a bad day things could get ugly.

I would imagine that refereeing is a job where it probably gets easier the more you do it, so perhaps we shouldn't feel too sorry for them. Conversely, as fans, we find that it doesn't get easier the more "mistakes" a referee makes. If anything it gets harder, and we get increasingly incensed and flustered with every perceived error.

Human beings are partisan and defensive in equal measure and this is never more true than when we are in a state of high emotion. In such critical instances the view we take of events is distorted heavily by our own emotional reading of the situation. From our seats, high above the action, squinting in the sunlight and with our view partially obscured by the flammable top hat in front of us, we believe that we can see every aspect of the game clearly and accurately. We actually think that our observations of an incident have greater precision and clarity than that of a full time professional referee who is standing just a few feet away from the action. When the referee then gives a decision that does not tie in with our interpretation, we throw our arms in the air and strop about like tired two-year-olds.

We know we were right – we saw it with our own eyes!

It is interesting to note, at this juncture, that the criminal justice system treats eyewitness testimonies as being among the most fragile and unreliable forms of evidence. There is a reason for this and that reason is down to the fact that eyewitness testimony is, at best, an account of what the witness believes to have occurred. Belief is a funny old thing. People believe some very strange things on the basis of very limited evidence. Just ask a fundamentalist Christian if you're in any doubt about that. If you thoroughly believe that your team is the team that should win (which is the stance taken by most followers of teams in any sport) then it will inevitably colour your understanding and interpretation of a critical event. You won't necessarily be aware of this, it just sort of happens subconsciously.

The result – you will be throwing your arms in the air, stamping your feet, frothing at the mouth and telling the world that this referee is useless, blind, inept, incompetent and overly fond of sexual self-satisfaction. Sound familiar? Or, if you are the sort of fan who is deeply insecure and paranoid, you will be claiming to have uncovered evidence of corruption.

"It's all part of the great anti-Wigan conspiracy," you will be saying to your chums who meet regularly, heavily disguised, in a darkened room to discuss the truth about the links between the assassination of Princess Di and the faked moon landings.

I would truly love to be a conspiracy theorist. Their world sounds so much more reassuring than mine. In my world things go wrong, for a start. Senseless mistakes happen, blunders occur and nasty accidents befall people with a terrifying lack of pretext. This is the hallmark of a random and uncaring universe. At least in the world of the conspiracy theorist you know that when something bad happens it is because some shadowy figure has meticulously planned it. That in itself provides some comfort.

For some people the possibility that referees might actually even be capable of making genuine errors is a terrifying prospect. Far better to curse them for their allegiances to other teams than to give credence to the notion that humans make mistakes.

"He did that because he supports Warrington" is easier for some people to stomach than the reality that we are a fallible species. The truth is that referees, despite what some would have you think, are human and that humans are prone to occasional clangers. It is impossible to think that any referee will be able to not make mistakes. Lapses, oversights and gaffes are bound to occur.

The Australians have tried to minimise this sort of thing by simply adding a second referee into the equation. Admittedly, for some this would just be compounding the issue – what could be worse than an incompetent idiot officiating the game? (Answer: two incompetent idiots officiating the game). It feels a little bit like an attempt to over-sanitise the game, but to some extent it has been a successful endeavour in terms of more effective policing of the play the ball area et cetera. I suspect we will soon be following suit over here. At least, we probably will when we've finally got enough professional referees to do so. It will not eradicate mistakes, though, because just bringing another human into the mix simply won't do that. It will just mean there is another person around capable of making mistakes.

Similarly, the video referee has propelled us into an era of slow-motion, high-fidelity, ultra-accurate, frame-by-frame analysis of the most important aspects of a game. With it we have the presence of the big screen at matches which has had the further effect of escalating our desire for knowledge. We now expect all the answers to be served up to us on a high resolution display.

I myself have fallen into this trap. I can no longer cope with not knowing stuff. The days when I could happily shrug my shoulders and resign myself to remaining ignorant are now but a distant memory. Sadly, this is not an indication of my possessing an ever-sharpening and increasingly enquiring mind. Quite the opposite – it is a sign of pure laziness. You see, now, whenever I am faced with something – anything – that I'm not sure about, my brain simply screams at me, "GOOGLE IT!"

This is my brain's response regardless of the nature of the question. Whatever it is, if it stumps me even just a little, then GOOGLE becomes my brain's default search engine. Even with seemingly innocuous questions, such as "how are you?", if I'm caught off guard then I find myself reaching for my smartphone and hoping there will be a 3G signal. I expect GOOGLE to provide me with answers to everything.

I suspect I am not alone in succumbing to this modern phenomenon of expecting to have answers to all things instantaneously available at the touch of a button. We have become so used to "factual" information being so readily obtainable at a moment's notice that we demand it in all aspects of our lives. It has to come quick and it has to be correct, otherwise there is hell to pay.

Consider in this the place of the poor beleaguered referee. If he deems it necessary to do a "square in the air" and call upon the assistance of the video referee then he is, in effect, instigating a delay in proceedings. This is the equivalent of a sudden loss of 3G signal. What might once have been swiftly concluded by a sequence of ambiguous nods between him and his touch judges will now take... literally...a few minutes.

For some fans this in itself is evidence that our full time professional referees are nowhere near as good as the referees of yesteryear.

"Fred Lindop would have sorted this out in seconds," they helpfully point out. It's true, he would. But the conclusion might have been considerably less accurate. In fact in the cases of some referees I can remember the conclusion would have seemingly been reached based on the alignment of the planets or the vagaries of the Mayan calendar (or perhaps a best guess based on a partially obscured view of what might potentially have been a try).

The video referee is supposedly less inclined to make decisions on the basis of astrological events and the whims of ancient civilisations. At the risk of upsetting those who like to think of the video referee as some all-seeing, omniscient and omnipotent entity, though, the video ref is not God. It's not even Stevo. I know this because on Sky Sports they have spent the last ten years emphasising that the video ref is not Stevo. Stevo himself is constantly saying it. He's not keeping a messianic secret – you can tell by the look in his eye.

So, on the basis that the video referee isn't even Stevo, then it can't be God either. The ontological argument for the existence of God supports this. According to the argument, God is the greatest thing that you can possible imagine. Well, I can imagine a lot greater than Stevo.

Fortunately we now no longer need to speculate on the exact nature and appearance of the mysterious video referee – the all knowing entity that is summoned with the sacred "square-in-the-air" gesture.

It's a couple of blokes in black bomber jackets stood in front of a big TV screen. While I can understand the reasoning behind Sky's urge to show us this scene (namely the drive for total transparency), I'm not sure that it has entirely worked out for the best. When people didn't know what the video referee looked like, they were free to imagine some kind of high-tech video editing laboratory inhabited by wise and judicious beings of unlimited intellect and an insatiable desire for truth and justice. Instead what we've been shown is a couple of confused doormen pawing at a TV screen in the same way that you sometimes see dementia sufferers trying to change the channel in the cinema. It just doesn't look good.

WORRY NUMBER THREE: THIS YEAR'S SHIRT.

Even to rugby league supporters, looking good is important. Prior to each new season there always seems to be a lot of angst about the team's appearance. The issue of the new playing strip is one of the foremost causes of concern amongst a significant number of fans, particularly during the off-season. What will next year's top look like? What shade of cherry will the red be? Do we want to go with the populist (if tacky) glace cherries, or are we better off with those posh dark ones? Will there be piping down the sides? Will it be black piping? Broad hoops? Skinny hoops? Traditional or new? Perhaps an old, traditional design from the days before colour TV that everybody has forgotten about – then it can be both traditional and new at the same time. What about the away strip? Blue, black or purple? Piping? Does purple piping show up enough on a purple shirt?

The fussing over the vagaries of a rugby shirt makes some supporters' conversations sound like a lover's tiff between Versace and Viv Westwood. All they seem able to agree upon is "Please, God, not the 'warrior rendered in vomit' motif of 1997!" In its defence I will say this of that shirt – it was coveted by my girlfriend of the time who was a London socialite working in one of the trendier youth departments of the BBC. I was only too happy to let her have mine. Provided she didn't stand near me when she was wearing it.

The more I think about it, though, the more I am convinced that the design of the playing kit is something that fans are quite right to be worried about. Because we wear the shirts too. Mostly we like to pick and choose our own clothes, but this is the one area where we sacrifice our sense of individuality along with any vestiges of haute couture we might have been clinging to. And in their place we usher in sartorial tribalism. Who wants to be a member of a badly dressed tribe? Look in your history books and tell me this – what happens to badly dressed tribes? I can guarantee that the answer is always the same. They get trounced by much nattier outfits.

Sleek Egyptians with braided hair and 1920s-style flapper dresses versus Hebrews in grungy desert chic: Egyptians win. German infantry in baroque gothic front-line wear versus clashing colours of the French army: away win to the Germans. Roman forces in metal/leather/kilt combinations versus raggedy Britons: Roman occupation. The evidence just continues to stack up against a naff home strip. Those same Romans versus wild-eyed, haggis-crazed Scotsmen in fetching tartan kilts: nil-nil draw on Hadrian's Wall. Don't try telling me the master tacticians and superior swordplay of the Scots kept the Romans at bay. It was those fancy kilts that saw them through.

I have just finished penning my fifteenth request in as many years to the Wigan chairman begging for common sense to prevail and for our team to take to the pitch in kilts. History says it would give us the edge. Sadly, the only reply I have ever had suggested that health and safety concerns prevent this from being a viable option. Ridiculous! Perhaps they are trying to tell me that kilts would be an open invitation to the likes of John Hopoate and Leon Pryce[20]. Or maybe they just want to keep the tackle free of flying tackle. They are missing the point, though. I'm not really suggesting that the team play in kilts. Only that they run out onto the pitch in them. Just enough to give history a little nudge in the right direction. To say…

"Here we are! We are warriors and we are well turned out! As such we are ferocious, determined and battle-hardened. We are men of pride and we are invincible!"

Then, in a movement inspired by Bucks Fizz's memorable 1981 Eurovision entry, they could rip off their kilts to reveal the regulation shiny shorts underneath. Before long folk from far and wide would be discussing the new "Wigan Haka". Surely that would be enough to put fear in the hearts of the opposition!

It has to be said that my advocacy of kilts has won me few friends among the supporters of our team. Most of

---

20 For those who don't know, in 2001 John Hopoate was found guilty of several incidents of inserting his finger into the backsides of opposition players. A few years later Leon Pryce was brought to book for repeated incidents of testicle squeezing during rugby games. And they weren't his to squeeze.

them simply turn their noses up at the idea and return to what seem to be more pressing matters of playing strip and replica shirt appearance. Once they have finished worrying about the style and colour of the shirt, they focus their attention on the sponsorship. Should we or shouldn't we have a major shirt sponsor? Should the shirts be available to supporters without the sponsor's logo? Should the logo be colour-co-ordinated to match the shirt? It opens up a whole new Heinz can of worms. I admit that I have also been guilty of worrying about this.

For instance, our new sponsor for the 2015 season is Coral. This brings a further level of anxiety into the question of whether or not I will be buying one for myself. The replica shirt used to be a guaranteed purchase every year, regardless of style or piping. But in these hard headed, recession-hit times I've become a bit more picky. There is now more discernment to my shirt shopping, and I'm just not overly comfortable with wearing the name of a gambling company on my chest. We've been here before. Back in 2010 I had similar concerns about having the "Mecca Bingo" logo adorned across my shirt. I've got all kinds of issues about gambling – an industry that some might say preys on the greed and hope of its paying clientele, whether they can afford it or not. As it happens, I have read through Coral's responsible gambling policy (available on the company's website, should you be interested) and I feel very much reassured. In 2010 my reservations were far more critical. Bingo is, after all, just another form of gambling. But there is a darker side to bingo, and I've seen it first hand – the look in the eyes of those bingo-crazed elderly ladies as the lust for victory (be it a cash prize or just a cuddly toy) takes over. They take it very seriously.

I once worked behind the bar in a Royal British Legion (an amateur set up, by Mecca's standards, admittedly) and the moment the bingo started, you made sure that you manned the bar in absolute silence. You did this out of a sense of pure terror. Even the slightest clink of glasses could be enough to incur the wrath of the grannies. More than a few clumsy bartenders had suffered unspeakable injuries as a result of an inadvertent bit of clinking. The things those old ladies could do with knitting needles just didn't bear thinking about. This is the effect that bingo has on the sort of ladies from whom the very worst you would otherwise expect would be a tickly kiss on the cheek. The question I had to ask myself was, "am I really going to allow my chest to become a moving advert for this phenomenon?"

And, as a teacher of Religious Education, could I have realistically considered wearing a shirt emblazoned with the name of the holiest city in the Muslim consciousness, which has actually been hi-jacked and used as an advert for gambling? Perhaps I was being unreasonable. Perhaps my thinking had been skewed by the nature of my job. Certainly no Muslim I know has ever voiced an objection to the Mecca logo. Personally, I don't like the connotations, but I have to admit that I cannot see any watertight objection on the basis of religious intolerance.

And I'm only too aware that to voice any such concerns would have left me wide open to criticism from those people who like to throw their arms in the air and shout "IT'S POLITICAL CORRECTNESS GONE MAD!" at every available opportunity. This is dangerous territory.

Political correctness (if you want to call it that) is not actually a bad thing, it is a very good thing. What *is* a bad thing are those people who, deliberately or not, bind political correctness to latent racism. Those people who feel it necessary to prefix completely acceptable observations with the words "I'm not being racist, but…"

The fact is, you are perfectly entitled to make observations about people, no matter who they are. You might even dare to generalise about people if you so wish, but if you do then you must recognise that you are leaving yourself wide open to argument. If, however, you apologise for your observation in advance of airing it, then what is that saying? By your own implication you are suggesting that there is something wrong with the person you are making your observation about. You regret having to say it, knowing the impact it will have. Or, even worse, you are voicing a sense of resentment about the fact that you have to be careful about what you say. You dislike having to be careful not to hurt people's feelings because it curtails your intention which is to be unnecessarily negative. So you say "I'm not being racist, but…" as a grumbling rider and to get your apology in first. Then you feel you can go ahead and be negative. But of course, it is not an observation then, it's an insult.

Far better, I think, to just go ahead and say it. If you don't mean to cause offence, then you probably won't. If you do, then at least it is out in the open and people will know exactly what sort of idiot you are.

Looking at it in this way, having "Mecca Bingo" written across your chest is actually totally innocent and isn't going to upset anyone. The same cannot be said, though, for the following post I once discovered on a rugby league internet forum. It was written by a Warrington supporter following his team's visit to play the Crusaders when they were still in the south of Wales.

"All we was doing, was walking down the street chanting, and the police said if we didn't stop they would arrest us for racism! Its another case of political correctness gone mad."

As for what they were chanting, well, it was pertaining to sheep. You can probably imagine what it was. So, basically, a man from England thinks that when he and his English friends are being prevented by the police from marching through the streets of a Welsh town repeatedly chanting the suggestion that Welsh men prefer the company of sheep to their wives, this is "political correctness gone mad."

A case of overly-finicky legislation.

He goes on to say:

"It was just banter, who would be upset by that?"

At this point he finds an observant ally.

"Yes, I saw a Welsh man laughing at it. What do the Political Correctness Brigade make of that?"

The Political Correctness Brigade? Who exactly are they? Are they a bit like the fire brigade, sliding down poles[21] and charging through the streets in the PC Engine, hosing down the fires of racist behaviour?

And then somebody else posted:

"Not being racist, but he was probably just laughing because he was looking forward to seeing his sheep."

Political correctness gone mad? No, racism is racism. No matter how funny you and your mates and the occasional bloke you see in the street find it, it is still racism. And because these people know that, and they know that they can't justify it, they hide behind phrases like "I'm not being racist, but…" and "Its political correctness gone mad!"

They do this because they think it makes them sound more acceptable. It isn't acceptable and it is merely the tip of a grim iceberg where comments about teams like the Crusaders are concerned. So much bitterness and resentment had already been voiced with regard to their position in Super League. The struggles in their first season were used as a vindication of the negative attitudes of many people, rather than being seen as obstacles that the club had to overcome. They should have been congratulated for sticking with it as long as they did, rather than being made to feel so unwelcome.

Latent xenophobia and racism certainly exists within rugby league. This is definitely something about our

---

21   Or Poles?

game that worries me. We are supposed to be a tolerant, accepting culture – more so than most other sports, especially when you consider the attitudes to our game that have prevailed over the years. The French Vichy Government is probably the most striking example. If any sport should have developed an all-embracing outlook, it is ours. Yet when we try to reach out and embrace others beyond our heartlands, be it the Crusaders, the Dragons or the Broncos, there are always a significant number of voices moaning about it. The call to protect our heartlands and drop expansion for no better reason than "they are not us" has an unpleasantly familiar taste about it. Yes, there are issues about accepting clubs into the top flight before they are ready, but expansionism is not merely a concept that can work, it is the only real means we have of propagating our sport. Sometimes, when an opportunity like the Crusaders comes along you just have to strike while the chance is there.

In any case, to get back to my original worry, I won't be buying one of the 2015 season's Wigan Warriors replica home shirts.

I'm not being racist, but I just can't stand black collars.

WORRY NUMBER FOUR: ARE YOU A GOOD ENOUGH FAN?

There are probably some people who would bring my claim to be a true Wigan fan into question due to my failure to invest in a replica shirt. In fact I know there are. I know these people exist because I have a lot of fun winding them up on internet forums. I have always taken a great deal of pleasure in playing around with people who take themselves too seriously. These are the people who are often the quickest to voice reasons why I and others like me cannot reasonably consider ourselves to be real, proper fans.

I don't buy the shirt, I don't sing all the songs, I don't attend every match, I don't stay to the end, I do clap the opposition, I do speak to opposition supporters...the list of behaviours that preclude me from being a "real fan" is almost endless.

I often wonder if the people who are so quick to judge have ever really thought about what a fan is.

On one level you could argue that it is better to be a supporter than it is to be a fan. A supporter, by definition, "supports" the club. That is to say that they are engaged in activities that will in some way benefit the club. They might offer financial support by, for example, attending games or by buying merchandise. They might in some way support the club's mission statement or provide further support by upholding the club's traditions.

On the other hand, a fan, by definition, is just a fanatic. This doesn't necessarily support the club, its mission statement or its ethos. I can get quite fanatical about all sorts of things without having to leave my bedroom. There is nothing noble about that[22].

---

22 Believe me, there really isn't.

Mind you, the self-appointed judges of fandom aren't talking about technical definitions. I'm not even sure that technical definitions are appropriate in these circumstances. It is an attempt to define the indefinable. It is like trying to calculate the radius of love. Somebody telling me that I am not a "real fan" because I don't stay behind to dance on the terraces at the end of a match is exactly the same as somebody telling me I don't love my children because I haven't taken them to Disney Land. It's meaningless.

I love this club. I love Wigan Warriors RLFC. I love Wigan in a very real sense.

I can say I love TWIX, and I probably mean it. But I have given up eating chocolate and I will probably never eat a TWIX again. I'm using the TWIX analogy to illustrate the difference between the sort of affection one has for confectionary and the sort of love I have for Wigan Warriors. I will never give up on Wigan.

I love my wife. I love Wigan Warriors. I'm never going to have sex with the Wigan team. No amount of Rohypnol, nor offers of an "Indecent Proposal" style from greying tycoons (so just be aware of this, Mr Lenagan) will ever make that an attractive proposition for me.

I love my family. All of them. Dearly. I can't always be there for them, but they are still family.

Love is a funny thing. It instils a sense of devotion that is almost as unfathomable as it is difficult to describe. Nobody will ever stand in judgement over my love of TWIX, my wife or my family. Quite simply, nobody is qualified to do so.

It strikes me as curiously odd, therefore, that there are people who feel qualified and compelled to stand in judgement over the love that I have for a rugby team. It is pure arrogance and it is the worst sort of navel gazing.

For what it's worth, my wife would never question my love of Wigan Warriors. She's a wonderful woman and I once stood in a building before both our families and all our friends and I promised to forsake all others.

As the vicar helpfully pointed out, forsaking all others doesn't just mean turning your back on old flames or potential new flames, but also forsaking all other friends, family members and recreational pursuits. From here on in, he was saying, your spouse comes first. What didn't help was that he then added,

"By the way, Matthew, that reminds me – I've booked our tickets for the semi-final."

Throughout my married life I have made a series of honourable compromises. The supporters who spot me sloping off a little early, or discover that I've watched the game from the comfort of my own living room don't like what they see. They get upset because I'm not fully in attendance.

How the hell do they think my wife feels? She has to cope with my repeated inattendance at our family home. Don't these people understand that my children occasionally want their daddy around on a Friday night and on Saturday morning? Don't they appreciate that if I leave the ground ten minutes early then that means I get home over an hour before I would have done otherwise?

And just let them dare tell me I'm not devoted to the cause when, during a Sunday afternoon family outing around Lacock Abbey, I'm desperately climbing trees in an attempt to find some mythical 3G hotspot so I can somehow tune in to BBC Radio Manchester.

Yes, I admit I've done it – I've been a Wigan Walker. When you've got a one hundred and sixty mile journey home ahead of you and the result of the game is a foregone conclusion, then leaving before the final whistle can make good sense. I get slightly irked by people who only have to roll out of bed to arrive at the DW Stadium telling me that my attempts to avoid the crowds leaving the area after the game render me inadequate as a supporter. Similarly, the fanatics who criticise others for not going to away games also manage to lodge themselves up my nose. Am I realistically going to make it to Hull by eight o'clock on a Friday evening? No. The train gets me into Wigan at ten to eight. That is after leaving Kemble at ten past four and keeping all fingers, arms, legs, toes and other dangly bits crossed in the hope that none of the connecting services are late. How dare people criticise my commitment, bearing in mind the time, expense and discomfort of the British Rail network? And don't even get me started on the interminable hell of the torturous inch-by-inch wrack they call the "M6". Sure, I could do that. But by the time I got to the match I'd be just as late as I would if I had taken the train. I'd also be deep in conversation with an army of invisible moon ferrets while randomly throwing my own excrement at passers by. That's what junction eight does to a man. I know because I've been there. Clearly this effort of passing into hell for a heavenly cause is not enough in the eyes of some for me to be considered a true fan. Not when I'm compared to those who stay to the end of matches and go to every away game. Of course, I'm just wallowing in my own circumstances. It is easy for an exile like myself to plead my case, but there are countless other followers of Wigan Warriors RLFC who have all kinds of reasons for arriving late and/or leaving early. How do you decide who the true followers of the team are? Simple – those who decide they are. I include in this my six year old daughter and infant son who will both jump and shout and scream and let off party poppers for every Wigan try they see on TV right up until their respective bedtimes. Neither of them has seen a full game, let alone visited the DW Stadium, and they won't for some time. Nevertheless, ask them whom they support and they'll tell you straight and true – "Wigan!" Support is like love. It lives in the heart and the soul, but not the navel. It manifests itself in different ways. Those who wish to impose their own attitudes, lifestyles and restrictions and codes on it are fooling themselves. The very best thing you can say about these people is that they are merely attempting to define the indefinable. You could also point out to them that they are displaying the initial signs of a tendency towards autocratic fascism. That's something best left amongst the navel fluff.

Perhaps, though, there is a suitable definition of what makes a good fan. Perhaps the answer lies in a retreat to those two terms – supporter and fanatic – and to marry them together. In so doing you create something positive. It is something that encapsulates the excitement of fanaticism while being true to the notion of support – of providing some form of benefit to the club. I suppose we call it being the "eighteenth man", because, when we're at our best, that is what we do. We provide something extra for the team. And we make a lot of noise.

I love a bit of noise as much as anybody else does. A rousing drum beat, a brass fanfare, the flags and the singing on the terraces – it's all great stuff. We can all get behind that. Number eighteen – the Wigan supporters in full pomp, spurring the team on. The wall of sound and the colour of the terraces. This, you would think, is an extremely positive dimension of fanaticism. And it is. It is a thing of beauty – a veritable work of art worthy of any gallery. Sadly, though, like any piece of artwork, it is not without vulnerability. Its beauty can be marred. In recent seasons we have witnessed the slow, steady rise of a small but vocal minority of Wigan fans who identify themselves as being "ultra"-fanatics. There is something about this, of course, that smacks of cultural elitism. There is also a more than faint sense of the ridiculous about them – attempting to be more fanatical than the normal definition of fanaticism has room for is a concept that seems ripe for a Monty Python style comedy sketch. But what is most worrying is that I recognise this pattern of behaviour from other aspects of life.

- Blind ideology? Check!
- Not prepared to concede or even consider an alternative point of view? Check!
- Overriding desire to be recognised as more devoted to the cause than other followers? Check!
- Inflated sense of self-importance? Check!

Yes, it's my old friend "religious fundamentalism". And when people start walking round with banners, concealing their faces with scarves and marching into opposition territories intent on intimidation, then it really is the darkest possible incarnation of fundamentalism. Of course, they claim that this is not the case. The old excuses fall lazily into place – "not breaking any laws," "exercising our right to speak out," "just showing a bit of pride..." et cetera ad nauseum. But pride, when it comes wrapped in identity-concealing apparel and starts jack-booting its way down your street under an aggressive emblem is something more than just a love of your club.

I suspect that the real love interest at play here is not for the game or for the team or even for the club as such. Rather, it is the notion of being an ultra-fan in itself that is the draw. It is fanaticism for fanaticism's sake by people who don't actually love the team but in fact just love the notion of fanaticism itself. They want to be noticed as being perceptively better at it than everybody else.

One of my favourite quotes is from the former Archbishop of Canterbury, Robert Runcie. He said "The

Church of England is like a swimming pool – most of the noise comes from the shallow end." I think it applies here as well. The radius of the love shown by those who use the cause to bestow status upon themselves is markedly skinnier than that shown by those for whom love is just love. I don't think I've written a deeper (or longer[23]) sentence in my life. It echoes the sentiments of one of my most favourite fictional characters – Kerr Avon – who said:

> *"I've never understood why it should be necessary to become irrational in order to prove that you care. Or indeed why it should be necessary to prove it at all."*

If he supported Wigan, he'd probably have been a very quiet fanatic, but on the inside he'd be doing triple backflips. That's love for you.

Of course, the noise itself isn't the issue. The problems arise when the activities of certain fans do not provide support for the club, but operate against the ethos, traditions and mission statement of the club.

That isn't being particularly supportive.

So what is a fan? Or a supporter? To my dismay, I think my wife best summed it up in what was probably meant to be a criticism of me.

"You spend far more time than is normal thinking about that bloody rugby team", she said. And, as usual, she was right.

---

23 My editor informs me that actually yes, I have. Frequently.

WORRY NUMBER FIVE: THE REST OF THE WORLD

I do spend a lot of time thinking about that bloody rugby club. I have done for as long as I can remember.

I've lived in exile since 1990 and keeping up with the latest Wigan news hasn't always been easy. There was a time when the high point of my week was the moment when a well-thumbed copy of the League Express would arrive on my doormat.

At some point – and for the life of me I can't remember when – things changed and suddenly the internet brought my obsession straight to me at the simple touch of a button.

It also opened the sluice gates to a torrent of unedited, undiluted and unrestrained opinion. It gave us all a platform for our views. I have always been fascinated to read the ethereal opinions, analyses and sentiments that are posted on internet forums for all to see. In a display of masochistic fascination that puts the Marquis De Sade to shame, I have taken a particular interest in reading what the supporters of other teams have posted about Wigan on the internet.

There is a lot of masochism to wade through but the following quotations seem to sum up the feelings of the fans of rival teams.

(Incidentally, although I haven't reproduced the quotes in full, I have retained the initial spelling and grammar in an attempt to preserve a sense of superiority, which is something that I think will please the authors of the comments. If nothing else, it will appeal to their somewhat distorted world-view. Needless to say that a liberal use of "[sic]" applies to these comments)."

> *"…we've got a long way to go if we are to be as despised as Wigan"*

- *"…As much as I don't like some of the St Helens players, I hate Wigan. In fact, We all hate Wigan, we all hate Wigan… Join in, you know the words."*
- *"…Just get over the bitterness and smile. We all hate Wigan, we all hate Wigan… Lets all laugh at Wigan… P.S Don't bother replying thanks."*
- *"…my new brother in law to be is from wigan, all his family are goons i hate them already…"*
- *"…every RL fan hates Wigan… coz you lot like to cheat a little."*
- *"… they're the ultimate establishment club…I loath their glory hunting, arrogant fans"*
- *"they are the scum mate…"*

I also found a whole Facebook page devoted to us. It described itself in the following terms:

Page Info

Short Description
basically just a hate campagne for the scum of the rugby league world!!

Long Description
everyone that hates the pie eaters should join and show theire support for the team thats playin wigan!

I hope I'm not jumping to conclusions, but I don't think that they like us. Bear in mind that all the above comments (and more) have been aired publically on internet sites for followers of a number of different teams. We seem to be the one thing that they all agree on. After hours of extensive research I could find no other team that seemed to provoke such a universal unleashing of hostility. My favourite discovery, though, was the emotionally charged diatribe printed below. It really is quite touchingly heartfelt.

The aforementioned "[sic]" rule applies doubly here.

"Not watched the superleague show as I don't need to know how Wigan RL have got away with stuff over the years , you've taken the game to the edge and over of fairness for 30 years so why would you stop now?...

...Irrespective of cheating the salary cap other clubs now copy what you do...you should be ashamed you cheating ba$tards!

Anyway Greg beat you at your own game and I can live with that day forever, all your other acheivements are hollow victories!...

...I'd put my salary on it that someone in Pieland is pulling the strings at Red hall as usual!

...Wigan nearly killed rugby league in the 80's... as much as it hurts to say – "Thank god for sky tv" but

> *thank a higher being for SALFORD RLFC putting an end to it! The games a much better spectacle without Wigan dominating/ruining it..."*

I read this with a smile right up until the "thank a higher being for Salford RLFC" line, at which point I literally howled with laughter. I was there at that cup tie in Salford when they turned their pitch into a suspiciously thin muddy swamp prior to beating Wigan. It was clearly a resounding victory for fair play and dignity.

There may well be plenty of things that we Wigan supporters should be worried about. But the one that is perhaps the most alarming is the way the supporters of Britain's other rugby league teams feel about us.

At least we can console ourselves with the thought that, no matter how neurotic we might be with our continuous Wigan Worrying, we don't worry half as much as the supporters of other teams do.

The difference is, they're all worrying about us.

Quite frankly, we're not popular. If you want it spelled out with a little more accuracy, we are almost universally hated. We are up there alongside the likes of Adolf Hitler, Justin Bieber and Katie Hopkins. We are the club that everybody in the world of rugby league loves to hate. In many cases they hate us with the same blinkered, fiery passion with which they love their own team. They sweat fury and spite for Wigan from every pore.

Sometimes such disdain for the club can take you quite unawares. For instance, a few years ago I was leading a group of teenagers on a Duke of Edinburgh Award Scheme expedition in the Peak District. I hopped dynamically over a stile to find myself face to face with an elderly couple who insisted on waiting and smiling as seven weary teenagers followed me over. I thanked this couple for their patience, but by this time they had clocked the 2004 Wigan away shirt I was wearing.

"You lot are bloody cheats!" spat the woman, cutting me off mid-sentence and pointing an accusatory finger at my chest. And then they were gone.

"Were they assessors?" asked one concerned youth.

"No," I replied. "They're worse than that. They're Castleford supporters." The kids took this at face value and we plodded on. But what sort of resentment must it take to taint such an innocuous meeting with that level of hostility? In front of children?

They really hate us.

Personally, I believe that if supporters of other teams could just manage to put their jealousy behind them for a little while, they might be able to recognise the fact that, if anything, they should love us. Perhaps even more than we do. It is indisputable that we have done them more favours than they realise.

Wigan have always had a strong away following and at the height of the team's success we were turning up to away games in numbers that had the chairmen of other clubs rubbing their hands together in glee. For those clubs clinging desperately to the cliff face of solvency, the prospect of a home thrashing by the Cherry And Whites was a win-win situation. Or rather, it was win-lose-(but win). And it might even have been win-maybe-actually-win-and-then-win-some-more. Because the worst case scenario would be that the Wigan entourage would turn up and fill the coffers as the team shredded the home side. Ker-ching! But there was also the prospect that the home side might actually beat the mighty Wigan (a prospect that in itself would encourage a few more home spectators to drag themselves to the game). If this happened, then it would have the added advantage of ensuring that their team's next few matches would be far better attended. In any case, win or lose, a visit from Wigan meant a financial shot in the arm. Surely they should be thanking us for this?

And that is before you even begin to consider all the other favours that Wigan has done for the world of rugby league over the years. As the first team to turn very nearly fully professional, Wigan effectively forced the hand of all the other clubs who aspired to greatness. Aspiring to greatness should be at the core of every club's mission statement. And Wigan led the way.

My next point is that Wigan have, over the years, provided some of the greatest PR opportunities that the sport has ever enjoyed. Take, for example, the code's most revered of competitions – the Challenge Cup.

Wigan made it famous.

As long as I can remember it has been a notable fixture on Britain's sporting calendar, but as Wigan's grip on the cup tightened over successive years, so the awareness of the competition grew in the nation's consciousness.

I have anecdotal evidence to support this view. Following Wigan's victory over Halifax in the 1987 cup final, I attended an event entirely unrelated to rugby league that was populated by people from all over the UK.[24] My attempts to spark up a rugby league related conversation[25] failed completely. Four years later, when I revisited the same event at the same location with, alas, pretty much the same dreary crowd, I chanced my arm again. This time eyes around the room lit up and there was much talk about "the cup that Wigan always win" and who might be the team to eventually depose them[26].

---

24 It was a Doctor Who convention, but I'm only prepared to reveal that to the sort of people who actually bother to read footnotes.

25 I wanted to know what my fellow "Whovians" would consider the most effective line-up for a rugby league team consisting of Doctor Who villains and monsters. Yes, I know how sad that sounds.

26 Infuriatingly the conversation became centred around Wigan's record in the cup and I never did have the in-depth discussion about a Doctor Who monster rugby team that I craved. But, for the record, here it is:
1) The Raston Warrior Robot (his positioning would be second to none) 2) Dalek (I once read that they can travel at speeds of up to 200mph which is just what you need on the wing – although I imagine at that speed, for a Dalek, cornering might be tricky. 3) Absalom Daak (only true Doctor Who fans know about him). 4) A Zaarbi (just because!) 5) Another Dalek. 6) Mr Sin (had to get him in somewhere). 7) The Master (for his never say die attitude). 8) Giant Robot. 9) A Sontaran (they look like hookers – and Stevo). 10) The Myrkha. 11) A Cyberman (very workman-like). 12) Hondo. 13) Agador.

Through its success, the club managed to provide the sort of advertising and public image for the sport that it would never have otherwise achieved.

I don't know, maybe we are the bad guys. It must be said, though, that it is hard to reconcile that thought with the evidence of the community work undertaken by the club and the general feeling of positivity about the place. I am prepared to admit that things didn't seem quite so squeaky clean in the Lindsay/Whelan era. Salary cap shenanigans and gunboat diplomacy seemed to be the order of the day, alongside an approach to the media that was often best summed up as "a pitbull in china shop". But even then I felt that the club was more guilty of mishandling issues than it was of being genuinely bad.

Let's not forget, Wigan were never found guilty of actually cheating the salary cap. The club just played to the rules in a way that wasn't within the spirit of the cap. The big money signing of Stuart Fielden in itself did not rescue Wigan from relegation. There are many people who insist that this deal was the one that broke the cap and effectively saved through the club through blatant cheating. Of course, Stuart Fielden contributed to the club's salvation, but he was just one part of the solution.

There were a number of different issues including an improved half back combination. If anything, the resurrected Kris Radlinski fit the bill as Wigan's saviour to a far greater extent than Stuart Fielden did. Had the club bothered to properly explain the circumstances around Kris Radlinski's payment then I'm sure that much of the criticism for this move would have been curtailed. I felt for Kris Radlinsksi. It was wonderful to see him back, truly it was. What saddened me was the talk amongst the supporters of other teams that seemed to imply some sort of mercenary attitude on his part. I have never met the man, but those qualities were never evident throughout his entire playing career. And before I am accused of being positively biased regarding the characteristics of all Wigan players, I can quite categorically state that I couldn't say the same for every player who has pulled on a Wigan jersey.

We must face facts. The fact is that Wigan RLFC have been a phenomenally successful club. Success will always breed jealousy and resentment.

So while we might have our own internal and familial heart wringing worries and wrangles over such matters as the signing of players, referees, playing strips and the nature of fandom, we shouldn't worry too much. As long as Wigan are top of everybody else's worry list then all is well with the world. It is where we always should be and I suspect it is where we always will be. They're all obsessed with Wigan to a degree that often puts my own obsession with the Warriors to shame. It's just not healthy.

This casts my mind back to my wife's perceptive description of what makes somebody a Wigan fan. And it's true for them too. They spend far more time than is normal thinking about this bloody club. Whether they like it or not, they're all Wigan fans too!

THE CUP-A-COASTER

My favourite ride in the whole wide world is The Big Dipper on Blackpool Pleasure Beach. This will never change. Ever.

Yes, before you ask, I have been on all those other roller-coasters that are dotted around the United Kingdom – Alton Towers, Drayton Manor, Digger Land et al. And they are all great. But there is something about that rickety old Big Dipper that I love. It might not go backwards or turn you upside down (unless you are very unlucky), it might not snap around corners with the break-neck speed of its modern counterparts, or dangle you by your ears over jets of water, but it still feels special to me. In particular I like the way it lulls the uninitiated into a false sense of security as it reaches its zenith and begins the descent. I love those few seconds of gentle downward gliding before the plunge. I will never forget my first time. Sat beside my father (who else?), full of trepidation, ratcheting our way to the summit together. As we started smoothly rolling down, I turned to my dad and flashed him a victorious smile. This, I was saying to him with that smile, is easy – I can cope with this and therefore I am now a man like you.

Seconds later I was curled up on the floor at his feet making a pitiful sort of "mmmnnnnnnnnnmmmmmg" noise as he howled with laughter.

Is the Challenge Cup not a bit like that? It starts so nicely and easily before dragging you helplessly on a journey of joyous ups, terrible downs and some pretty sickening corners. It is the Big Dipper by another name. A good rollercoaster requires an act of courage. It asks you to put yourself in a position where you feel a little bit unsafe. You have to take a leap of faith. It also fizzles with excitement. From the very moment you lock yourself into your seat, you know that something special lies ahead. You know that at times your animalistic instincts will scream for release while the more rational voice of your higher reasoning will howl in wide-eyed enjoyment as adrenalin surges through your system. Somewhere on that ride you reach a special moment when the ecstasy of flight is met by the opportunity for disaster and the effect is electric.

It is an effect that, in sporting terms, you only really see in a true knock-out competition. This is what the Challenge Cup delivers. It is a tumultuous roller-coaster ride of a competition and it is available to the nation through the glorious institution that is the British Broadcasting Corporation.

My love for the Corporation is akin to my love of rugby league itself. It is a wonderfully robust and adaptable national treasure that we should all hold dear. And like rugby league, it is not afraid to innovate.

The news that the BBC was relocating the bulk of its operations to Salford might have come as a harrowing jolt to the more genteel Londonphiles among its workforce, but I'm sure I wasn't the only rugby league enthusiast to greet this move as a truly positive development. As soon as I heard the news, I felt a distinct shiver of excitement. It seemed to me that having the BBC so deeply ensconced within a rugby league city like Salford could only work in our favour. Surely rugby league would permeate the sensibilities of the BBC policy makers, even if it was just on a subconscious level. In fact they wouldn't even have to make any sort of purposeful effort to value the game more, it would just happen by association. They were coming North, these BBC bigwigs, they would get rugby league in their blood. By osmosis. I considered that it might take a little time but sure enough, the movers and the shakers at the Beeb would eventually be moving and shaking at the prospect of a Challenge Cup tie in much the same way as it gets me moving and shaking (namely my bowels and hands[27]).

If ever rugby league needed a strong Salford club, then this is the time. It is, therefore, something of a relief that Salford has been rescued from its former precarious position by Doctor Marwan Koukash. He has done the sport a great service. Admittedly, he does look a little bit

---

27 One moves and the other shakes.

like a villain from a casted-by-numbers[28], second rate attempt at a Bond movie. He is, however, a genuine saviour. I expected the rugby league press office to make a little more mileage out of that.

The RFL governing body should be throwing everything they've got at accommodating the Salford team's status and position. They should be subsidising tickets for young spectators and families, throwing on free pie and peas for pensioners, buying up the advertising billboards closest to the BBC media village and introducing clever poster campaigns depicting Salford players in Lowry-style paintings (they would love this, those BBC chief executives, because it would speak to them of culture and northern chic). They should be doing absolutely anything and everything. Except, of course, for re-releasing the "Red Alert" single of the late 1990s.

In all fairness, the BBC has generally done us proud. In days gone by, when people were simpler in their tastes and were still experimenting with "squarials" it seemed like everybody had at least a passing interest in the Rugby League Challenge Cup. Let's make no bones about it, that interest was fostered by the BBC's coverage. We owe them a huge debt. From the Floodlit Trophy to the Challenge Cup, they have been the most successful advertising agency we have ever cosied up to. I shall always maintain that a broadcasting network funded by a government-regulated licence fee is a stroke of pure genius. As rugby

---

28 Or, perhaps, "casted-by-prejudices".

league supporters who pay our licence money, we are entitled to representation. That's a powerful tool. We know that Sky cherish rugby league because of the healthy viewing figures the sport procures, and that is fair enough. But there is always going to be some statistical skewing in their viewing figures as long as some people are buying Sky subscriptions on the sole basis that they are rugby league fans. The Super League coverage is the only reason I tolerate a Sky dish on my chimney and I imagine there are many others who buy into the satellite network for the same reason. Sky stick with rugby league because it makes financial sense for them to do so. The BBC, on the other hand, simply cannot ignore us. Certainly, it has always been the case that the quality of our "product" has attracted viewers regardless of geographical association. Think of rugby union and flip that on its head. If the roles were reversed and the other code didn't enjoy its national cultural supremacy, how many people would find themselves glued to it as a result of accidentally tuning in on a Saturday afternoon?

We know the answer. But the fact remains that our presence on the BBC is the key to our presence in the national consciousness. Due to the nature of the licence fee the BBC has a pressing mandate to show rugby league. For the BBC it is a matter of moral ideology as much as it is a financial decision. This appeals to me enormously.

Add to this the fact that every public house in the country has access to the BBC, and we are close to unearthing the core of my fondness for the Challenge

Cup. I can pop into my local village pub and watch Challenge Cup fixtures in there because, due to the BBC coverage, it is by far the most accessible competition we have.

Of course I could watch it at home. But if I am not able to attend a game then my preference is to watch it in a public place because I can always guarantee at least one convert and a few others who will at least be tempted to watch another game.

Pubs that, unlike my local, do have Sky TV are often more guarded about watching rugby. On a Saturday afternoon you can ask a landlord to switch on BBC in order to watch "the rugby" and they will do so without question if they don't have Sky Sports. The landlords of pubs that boast a satellite dish will be a bit more sceptical.

"Which rugby?"

"Who is playing?"

"Suppose it upsets the customers?"

"We watch football here."

I suppose if you are paying for a service with one particular sport in mind when you make your purchase, then it makes you a bit more skittish about what appears on your screen.

The pubs without Sky tend to be more grateful of any televised sporting event. Besides, when you ask someone to tune in to the BBC then they automatically feel that what is being transmitted is worthy of the general viewing public.

The admiration I have for the BBC is by no means limitless though. This is evidenced in a letter I wrote to

the BBC following a particularly disappointing cup draw
not too long ago.

Dear BBC,

Hello. I am a devoted fan of the Wigan Warriors (a
rugby team from the northern region). You will notice,
I hope, that within my bracketed description of the
aforementioned team, I declined to use the word
"league" as a suffix to "rugby" to provide further clarity
with regard to the exact nature of the sport played by
the Wigan Warriors. I did this purposefully for the sake
of brevity. I feel certain that, as a very busy broadcasting
institution, you will appreciate me not wishing to waste
your time with unnecessary wordage. We both know that
the word "league" would have been totally redundant in
this context, don't we? As soon as I mentioned "Wigan"
your gestalt institutional hive mind immediately made
the association with the thirteen man code.

That is because we go way back, me and you. We
have history together. You brought me my earliest
memories of televised rugby and you have provided me
with a staple diet of scintillating rugby league action in
the form of the Challenge Cup. We've shared so much,
haven't we? And down the years we've always been
there for each other – me with my licence fee and you
with your coverage.

Let me talk about the licence fee for a moment. Back
in 1995 when I first paid it (and we shall not speak of the

179

"confusion" regarding the payment of said fee during my years as an undergraduate student in Wales – the Welsh themselves seem unclear regarding their membership of the United Kingdom, let alone the notion of Britishness and therefore the funding of the BBC is a fuzzy area in Wales. Besides, I was in a communal hall of residence – we were all practically sharing the same ariel/coathanger. I had it on Tuesdays as I remember…)

I digress, where was I? Oh yes. Back in 1995 the licence fee cost me exactly £86.50. Ten years later it cost me £126.50. It now costs me £145.50. Nothing about this has ever surprised me or struck me as being unfair. Indeed, I expect the fee to adapt to rising production costs and inflation. Let's call it "moving with the times," shall we?

Now let me talk about your coverage of the Challenge Cup. If we're honest, it hasn't always been quite as adept at moving with the times, has it?

Oh, I'm not decrying the entertainment value you've provided over the years. Thrilling heroics, tantalising tries, pineapple rings and prime ministers – it's been a tremendously enjoyable ride. But you had it all served up to you on a plate, didn't you?[29] All you had to do was point your camera and press "REC". Ok, so maybe you had to provide editing and commentary and national distribution through your impressive broadcasting network, I understand that.

---

29 Admittedly, this wasn't how the pineapple ring was served.

But if we're looking at ourselves honestly and critically, do we think we could have possibly done a bit better? I say "we", but I'm actually talking about "you", not "me" – I'm keeping my end of the bargain, my licence fee is set up on a direct debit and I'm pretty sure that suits both parties to perfection.

Sometimes, not always, but sometimes, the overall impression that BBC coverage has left the casual viewer with is that rugby league is the sporting equivalent of the end of the pier show. Blackpool Pier, that is, as opposed to the far more cultured and cosmopolitan ambience provided by your Brighton Pier.

In other words, sometimes you make us feel like Cannon & Ball's desperate last appeal to a diminishing and increasingly tired audience. Once or twice, in the earlier rounds, you have even made us feel like Little & Large. Fairly recently, during a live cup draw on 5live, you even made us feel like The Chuckle Brothers. We do know that we are, mostly, a northern sport. We're aware of that. We are also aware that there is a small but significant hard core of truth at the centre of every stereotype. Otherwise they wouldn't be very good at being stereotypes. They would be unstereotypical and would instantly lose any cultural recognition that they once owned. And they wouldn't be anywhere near as funny.

But let's not get sidetracked into a discussion of the semantics of political correctness. The fact is that you don't have to resort to excessively milking the cow of northern subculture in order to make our game appealing to the general public. I think you'll find that we are already providing you with the cream of the sporting crop. Our game is fast, furious, hard-hitting and quite frankly amazing. It doesn't need any extra "Eeeh Bah Gum". Its got "Eeeh Bah Gum" aplenty already.

What it does need is a little spring cleaning in the visual presentation department. I'm not asking you to flood the screen with unintelligible, throbbing graphics in the way that some broadcasters seem to feel is necessary. I don't need any more of that. If I want my rugby coverage to look like a technicolour Christmas tree on an acid trip, then I know exactly where to go, thank you very much. To the discerning viewer such an approach raises the suspicion that beneath all the tacky icing, the cake is just a digestive biscuit. Our game is not a digestive biscuit and we need little in the way of icing.

What would be nice would be a few more camera angles. You know, to make it look like we're not watching the game on the stadium's security cameras.

I am being a little cruel, but I think we've known each other long enough for real candour to be permissible. I know you so well, BBC. I have snooped around your most private areas on many occasion when my ex-girlfriend (an employee of yours) allowed me access to your TV Centre, I saw first hand how you cling to outdated, archaic infrastructures and bureaucratic systems. Its one of the reasons I feel so drawn to you and so comfortable in your presence. You don't like to mess with history and tradition. You look at the Challenge Cup and you see history and tradition running through its veins, hence your reluctance.

I must urge you, though, that the time has now come for an update. I know you can do it, BBC. I know you've got it in you to revamp your coverage while still being true to the competition's rich heritage. I don't know how you're going to do it, but I do I have every faith in you.

I'll leave that one with you.

Best wishes,

Matt Macaulay

PS. Tell Andi Peters I'm sorry about the time I was sat at his desk when he walked into his office, but he didn't need to be so stroppy about it. He's just bitter. He'll never be Brian Kant and he knows it.

On one level I can certainly understand the BBC's reticence when it comes to innovation. Messing with the Challenge Cup can feel a bit like messing with history itself.

The Challenge Cup is the purest of competitions. There is something illustrious and wholesomely archaic about its very nature. From the outset when the first ball is pulled from a bag in a room filled with anticipation, it feels like a competition that is alive and vibrant. Its lifeblood throbs in the veins of our sport, energising its most distant limbs with the oxygen of heritage. I mention the draw in particular because it in itself is a beautiful thing that brings health and vitality into every muscle, vessel and organ in the body of the game. All achieved with the humble and meagre act of plucking of a few balls from a bag.

But in some quarters there is much consternation about the state of our balls. Amongst the conspiracy theorists there is talk of hot balls, cold balls, hard and squishy balls. Suggestions are rife that those pundits who have been selected to make the draw have been well drilled in the dark art of selecting the correct balls. In short, there is a growing lobby of rugby league cynics who are convinced that the draw for the televised cup rounds is fixed. I am somewhat bemused by this assertion. As far as I can tell this murky suggestion is quite literally a load of balls. I mean, why would anybody do that? Which devious super-villain is sitting in his lair, stroking his white cat and cackling as teams are drawn from the bag to his evil satisfaction? Is it Doctor Koukash?[30]

If such nefarious acts were being conducted behind the scenes, it is hard to understand why. It's not even as if these "fixed" draws are resulting in a series of games between perfectly balanced sides. Part of the charm of the Challenge Cup lies in the clearly evident

---

30   I can genuinely picture it.

fact that sometimes you do see one-sided games with poor attendances live on television. This doesn't really seem to bother anybody apart from a certain section of the game's devotees. Plainly the BBC does not seem overly concerned about it. But, conversely, how concerned might the BBC be upon discovering that one of their valued sporting competitions was rigged, with or without their knowledge? Massively concerned, I should think. And it really wouldn't matter whether the BBC knew about it or not. They didn't even have to name a leading member of the Conservative Party who potentially might have been involved in a North Wales children's home sex abuse scandal. The mere fact that they interviewed somebody who later did so on Twitter was deemed damning enough. Even worse, the tabloids had a field day a few years ago when it appeared that Ant and Dec had robbed everybody's 'phone money on behalf of ITV. Is this really the sort of environment in which a national broadcaster would happily encourage or even turn a blind eye to rigged draws? Somehow I doubt it.

Maybe I'm being naïve. Maybe it has always happened and always will until we come up with some infallible way of making a random draw live on television. Everybody seems to trust the National Lottery draw which takes place live on television every week. It might be that the answer lies with machines. The key to dispelling any fears regarding the legitimacy of the draw for Challenge Cup fixtures could well be to have a see-through Genevieve regurgitating balls live on air[31]. And if that's what it takes to silence the cynics, then so be it.

There is probably very little point in worrying about this sort of thing. Not when there are more important things to worry about – things like the fixtures themselves, for instance.

You literally don't know who you're going to get. This doesn't happen at any other stage in the rugby league year. Super League fixtures are laid before you well before the start of the season, giving you the chance to get your head set in anticipation of the year's coming highs and lows. Even the play-offs are chosen from a limited field and according to a format and structure that gives you some idea of what is coming your way. The Challenge Cup, on the other hand – and particularly the earlier rounds (up to the start of the 2015 season) – could and would throw up literally anything. It is the leap of faith. It is the moment of courage as you step into the rollercoaster car.

It is a true knock-out competition and it has a number of rather curious effects on my behaviour and physical well being.

---

31 This may sound like some extreme form of adult entertainment experience that should be confined to dodgy freeview channels in the wee, small hours but I swear that I have seen it on BBC before the watershed. Wait 'til the Murdoch papers get hold of that (fnar!).

Ask me how I feel.

Go on, ask me how I feel during the build up to Challenge Cup tie. I'll tell you. My body physically betrays my anxiety.

Let's start with my legs. My legs twitch. They do it for days on end. Both of them – they're in cahoots. There I will be, doing something entirely inert (which is pretty much my default setting) such as sitting in a pub, reading a paper and nursing a pint when suddenly, without warning, my left leg will begin to twitch of its own accord. It happens slowly at first – an almost imperceptible trembling against the table leg – but gradually the strength and the momentum will build to a leg-vibrating crescendo until what I'm doing against the table leg looks like a cross between footsy and fire-lighting. If this doesn't freak the locals out, I can guarantee they are certain to react by the time my right leg gets in on the act. Sooner or later somebody will decide that enough is enough and ask the bar staff to remove the "odd grasshopper man with the smoking table leg clamped between his knees" from the premises. At this point I will be forcibly ejected onto the street. Still twitching. And it's not just my legs, either. The state I am in is not restricted to my lower extremities. It is not the case that my legs are kicking wildly while my upper body remains dormant (just in case you were thinking I suffer from sort of involuntary River Dance syndrome). As lovely as that might sound, that's not it. Because my arms are active too. They are reaching out and grabbing things, fiddling restlessly with them, my fingers endlessly tracing contours and wrapping themselves around all kinds of random objects. And then there's my face, which is also afflicted. My mouth goes mad. My lower jaw unshackles itself and launches[32] an audacious attempt to eat the rest of my head.

Riverdance, cleptomania and gurning all at once. I'm difficult to miss as I lurch awkwardly down the street. But this is not the normal me. I'm not usually like this. It is an affliction that is solely due to the imminence of a particularly gripping Challenge Cup game. For example, a game like a quarter final tie away at Warrington. The symptoms aren't just physical either. I experience sleepless nights, laying on my back and going through various team selection and tactical interchange permutations in my head. I also exhibit various different signs of stress and emotional fatigue. I snap at my wife and children, cower from anything that is vaguely similar to the colours of the opposition team. On top of this, I lose the ability to concentrate on anything for more than a matter of minutes.

I loathe the inexorable period of emotional and mental torment prior to cup games. I want the moment of kick-off to arrive immediately, not merely because I will enjoy the game, but mainly because I hate the agony of the wait. I wish away days of my life. And to put this into perspective it should be noted that I am a school teacher who is often on his summer holidays during

---

32 Or "lunches", if you will.

the latter rounds of the cup. I quite regularly wish away chunks of my life during term time. Most of my students also wish chunks of my life away during term time – it's very common. But not during the holidays! To wish your holidays away is anathema to teachers. Yet quite regularly during the summer I find myself stabbing at the fast-forward button to Saturday 2.30pm, or whenever the kick off might be.

Back in 2011 Warrington did actually host us for a quarter final tie in the Challenge Cup. I remember that as being a particularly torturous build up prior to the game. It was possibly one of the worst kinds of Challenge Cup ties you could get,

There are some teams you just know you are going to beat. Admittedly, quite often Wigan don't actually beat them (and who can forget leaving the Halliwell Jones Stadium after that Catalans game a few years ago – abject misery, compounded by the Wolves supporters who had lined the streets to wave us home). But that's not the point. You are going to be either elated or despondent after a cup game, you know this and you deal with it. The fact is, you don't worry yourself sick in the build up because you feel, deep down inside, that you are going to win. Supporters of other teams will try to persuade you that this is a purely Wigan thing – a pie eater's conceit. They're telling lies. It's far from being just a Wigan thing, its a common human flaw experienced by everyone from Oedipus to the captain of the Titanic. We have all at some point been slightly complacent because we feel like we are in control, when actually we aren't. Quarter-finals against teams you "know" you are going to beat are relatively stress free. As are cup games against teams who you just "know" are going to beat you. That happens too. As those balls are plucked from their velvety bags by whichever former players have been roped in to act as the teasing harbingers of fate, as the names of teams are read out, there are times when your heart plummets like a stone. So you breathe a big shuddering sigh before consoling yourself with the thoughts that:

a. at least you will be saving yourself a bit of money, and
b. your team can now concentrate on the league.

There may be some truth in (a). You may well save yourself a bit of cash by not travelling to Wembley. Sadly (b) is rather more problematic because all you've done there is shifted your emotional eggs into one basket having previously had them in two baskets. Yet you hang in there until the point where you say to yourself, following another shuddering sigh, "well there's always the Internationals – England are looking good for once!" To be followed closely by "oh well, I'm a Wigan fan at heart, and now I can just concentrate on next season."

I have deviated from the point. There are two good types of cup games. These are the ones you know that you are going to win and the ones you know that you are going to lose (admittedly these are less good, but easier in terms of damage limitation).

Then there are games against teams like the Warrington side of 2011. It was a game Wigan could win. It was also a game Wigan could lose. That's what I don't like because it always fuels a torrid fire of anxiety within me.

To make matters worse, the BBC have a policy of declaring any team who face us to be the "underdogs." That makes us the perennial "overdogs" and straight away I don't like that at all. It brings to mind the exact same ironic way in which Shaun Edwards used to declare Wigan to be the underdogs in the build up to cup matches during those eight glorious years. And now we'll never be the underdogs again. All because of those eight consecutive cup final victories, not to mention our previous illustrious record. Thanks to that we'll always be the "Cup Kings" or the "team whose name was synonymous with Wembley." We are practically establishment, and nobody wants the establishment to win. On the contrary, everybody wants the underdogs to rise up and bite the establishment where it hurts. Just like on every Hollywood blockbuster ever made, and sadly we are now the bad guys. We are the Empire in "Return of the Jedi", Mr Potter in "It's A Wonderful Life," and Hydra all rolled into one. It doesn't matter how well other teams are playing or how good St Helens, Warrington or Leeds recent records are. It is going to take us a lot longer than two decades to shift our tag.

It also means that not only are the opposition supporters hoping we fail, but so is every supporter of every other team and every neutral viewer the BBC can pull in with its (sadly limited) advertising. They are all against us.

They won't go easy on us if we do lose. There will be little in the way of humility shown by the victors, their supporters or the neutrals. It will be a gloat-a-thon. It always is. I'm not entirely sure that we deserve this treatment. I'm certain that I don't because I always make a point of applauding the other team's efforts, and I will clap any try that is scored well. I think of myself as a very gracious Wigan supporter. Nonetheless, should Wigan lose then I too will be subjected to howls of derision and scorn during the short walk between the stadium and my car after the game. This will be followed by endless ribbing and taunting on the internet message boards and the sort of smug, self-gratifying mockery that permeates the thickest of skins and puts scabs on your soul.

That is what happens when teams like Wire beat us. There is always a tide of Warrington vitriol (tempered only by the joy and relief of victory) rolling towards Wigan like the Severn Bore when we lose. But who can blame them? Most Wigan supporters still have the satisfying taste of almost continuous Wembley victory lingering at the back of the throat. By stark contrast, the throats of Warrington supporters are dry, parched and cracked, with barely the dry vapours of success lingering in their airways. I can only imagine what the opportunity of another cup final at Wembley would mean to them. I suppose on the occasions when the likes of Warrington do beat us in the cup, perhaps they could probably be forgiven an over-zealous response.

Of course, we do tend to win more than we lose.

But ask yourself this – which is worse? Never to have tasted victory (in which case, through the application of pure logic, you would therefore be oblivious to the pleasure you are missing out on, like Warrington were) or to have that faint, glorious taste in the back of your throat, and yet to be denied another bite? Now that really is torturous. That goes beyond the cruelty of day-to-day existence – it is the sort of technique that would not seem out of place in the darkest chambers of Camp X-Ray. Forget the thirst of Warrington supporters – we deserve to win. Or, at the very least, we deserve not to lose. Not if there is any supreme power of good in the universe. Not if there's a god.

This possibly seems like a rather extreme statement to make – that Wigan not reaching the Challenge Cup Final would in some way provide evidence for the non-existence of god. Coming from a vicar's son, as it does, this could almost seem blasphemous (although I suspect my dad would be on my side). Is it right to risk blasphemy on account of a cup match in a competition that has, in recent years, been clearly diminished and starved of light as it is forced to seek an existence in the shadow of the Super League Grand Final?

The answer is a resounding "yes!" Perhaps I speak only as a Wigan supporter who once came to view Wembley and London as a home away from home. But the fact remains, I retain the deepest affection for the Challenge Cup. I often wonder why.

The sudden-death element of the competition is

certainly one explanation for our love affair with the Cup. We Wiganers do love living on the edge and sailing close to the wind. As supporters who have experienced more than our fair share of the glory, we appreciate that the highs are so much more potent when you're surfing the frothy cusp of the wave. True, we also feel the hurt of the wipeout more than most others, but we know that the rewards make the risk worthwhile. And the risk makes the rewards sweeter.

The other reason is that we still think of that cup as ours. We might not have seen as much of it as we would have liked in recent years, but it still belongs to us. Not in a materialistic sense, though. More in the manner of an ex-girlfriend who keeps coming back to us because we were her first love. She's been with other clubs, but we know that while she sits in their dusty display cabinets, she's really thinking of us. When she is with those other clubs she is a damsel in distress, imprisoned in a glass coffin. At least when she comes to Wigan she feels at home. She can get some ironing done and pop down to the Co-op in her slippers.

It is, therefore, our mission to rescue her. We are her knights in cherry and white armour, annually renewing our mission to deliver her safely from the clutches of those unsuitable suitors who pretend to love her, but really they only want the cash. It is our duty of chivalry to bring her home.

We may not always succeed, but the failure of one year makes the success of the following year all the sweeter.

True love waits, and we will wait for her until the day Hull freezes over, if need be. She will wait too, but she is a woman so she will only wait on the condition that we are actually slogging our guts out to get her back. Unconditional love is a notion alien to women and silverware. This is the nature of our special relationship with the cup. We love it.

We love cup final day too. I think all rugby league fans do. It is our sport's day in the sunshine. Rugby league going south always carries with it the spirit of missionary work. We converge on London en masse in a surge of evangelic zeal.

As fans of a sport that has (and does still) face discrimination on grounds of class and culture, we are never so happy as when we march on London. I know what these southerners say about us. I hear the same thing time and time again. They think we're dying. They consider us to be an anomaly, clinging on to the precipice of extinction.

Other "niche" sports aren't viewed this way. Like us, they are frequently patronised and belittled, but nobody rubs their hands in glee while predicting the slow, agonising death of ice hockey or speedway racing in the UK. They are allowed to be what they are – professional sports making their way in the world.

We suffer from three main problems. Firstly, we are a separate code of a well-established sport. That well-established sport has the advantages of money, power and influence. Naturally the Rugby Football Union doesn't like us – nobody likes to look at a morally superior version of themselves, it's quite unsettling.

Our second problem is the fact that we have never really successfully expanded. I say this with some trepidation, because actually we have. If you look at the draws for the early rounds of the Challenge Cup you will see we are a truly national (and international) sport. My nearest team is actually a lot nearer than I had thought it would be – Swindon St George are located a few miles down the road. The Gloucester All Golds are a few more miles up the same road.

Sadly, though, we are still perceived as a sport confined to touching distance of the M62. That brings with it all the usual stereotypical images of northerness. As long as southerners continue in the erroneous view that the north is a dying wasteland, then they will continue in the erroneous view that our sport is also dying.

Our third problem is that we are ambitious. We want to take on the world. We want to stage world cups and world club challenges, and we're always seeking the bigger stage. Sadly, ours is a society where small fish are scorned for daring to harbour ambition. Every cup final or international game we stage is fraught with our fourth problem (I didn't want to mention it earlier because three problems seemed quite dismal enough) – the chip on our shoulder. We are always looking for the negative in our sport. Why wasn't it a full house? Why was the game not quite as exciting as it could have been? Why does the world hate us? When we dwell on the downsides it is hard to criticise everybody else for following suit.

We may well have much to be concerned about, but our annual invasion of the country's capital is our clearest opportunity not only to showcase the thrilling nature of our game, but also to let the world know we are in rude health. It is our version of the storming of the Bastille.

Besides, you know what cup final day is like – it's sunny and festive. Even in the pouring rain. It is two of our top teams battling it out in the midst of celebration and summer fun. What's not to love? You can't possibly be miserable on Cup Final day, at least not until your team loses. Even then, there is always the carnival atmosphere to cheer you up – and it most certainly will. The Rugby League Challenge Cup really is all the fun of the fair.

PIES, DAMNED LIES AND STATISTICS

Every third car you see today will be silver. It's a popular colour. One accepted reason for this is that many drivers equate silver with wealth and status. However, this does not necessarily mean that everybody you see driving a silver car is rich and famous. They just want to give that impression. Statistics, you see, are tricky little fellows. It is probably more accurate to say that everybody you see driving a silver car will be wearing driving gloves, sitting on a seat cover fashioned from wooden beads and carrying (usually in the glove compartment) a bag of Werther's Originals and a round tin containing travel sweets coated in a fine dusting of what looks suspiciously like cocaine powder. This is because, regardless of recent trends, silver has always been the car colour of choice for elderly men.

Is every third car driven by an old man, though? In Ormskirk, yes. Otherwise no.

From this we can surmise that Ormskirk is full of old men and that, due to the higher number of road traffic collisions attributed to elderly drivers, Ormskirk is an accident black-spot. But it isn't. As I mentioned earlier, statistics are quite tricky.

Two people are killed by vending machines every year. What does this tell us? It suggests that for the most part vending machines are fairly placid machines (especially when compared with, for instance, Terminators or Daleks). On the face of it, it is much better to have a vending machine serving your hot beverages than a Dalek. However, you should still be wary, because should you upset a vending machine then it may well kill you. There are no statistics available for the number of minor injuries inflicted by vending machines which suggests that these things don't mess around. If they're upset, they'll murder you. Outright. No warning nudges or shots across the bow, just the simple, cold vending of sudden death.

Men think about sex once every seven seconds. This means, alarmingly, that whenever I talk to a man on the terraces at a rugby game, at some point during our conversation (assuming it lasts longer than seven seconds, which I appreciate is not necessarily the norm at many rugby grounds) he will think about sex.

The bastard.

He doesn't respect me or my conversation. He's only after one thing. Mind you, I'm a man too and by the same token this means that I will also be thinking about sex once every seven seconds. So I probably shouldn't be too harsh on him. I wonder if we ever synchronise? Whether there is a seventh second during our conversation when we are both thinking about sex? That could lead to an embarrassing pause. Maybe all embarrassing pauses in conversations between men are down to "seventh second sex synchronisation syndrome".

I hope not.

Two thousand and five hundred left handed people die every year while trying to operate right handed implements. This really scares me. I am left handed and, it has to be said, I'm not the most dextrous of individuals. Even for a lefty I'm hideously clumsy. I am so clumsy, in fact that I fail to see how I'm going to manage to effectively accidentally kill myself with a right-handed can-opener. That's how inept I am. I think it would need to be a fairly prolonged bout of accidental can opening. And I would have to be in a pretty determined frame of mind – almost obsessively desperate to open that can. Even then, logically speaking, the parts of my anatomy most at risk would be my fingers. And once every single one of my fingers was lying on the floor, I would probably be inclined to stop can opening. Even if I wasn't so inclined, it is hard to envisage how I would continue.

So should I really be so wary of right-handed can openers? I've never really been scared of them in the way that I am scared of, for example, man eating crocodiles. Are they more or less dangerous? How many left handed people are killed every year by crocodiles? Considerably fewer than 2500 is the answer. It is official – for us left handers, can openers are more dangerous than crocodiles. This, for me, is the best thing about being left handed. While "righties" creep terrified through crocodile-infested swamps at their peril, I can splash gaily through those same swamps without a care in the world. Unless, of course, one of those crocodiles happens to be carrying a can opener, in which case I am literally up the creek.

Twelve percent of lightning strikes occur on golf courses. This doesn't bother me. I don't play golf – it would be too dangerous, what with me being left handed and everything.

Judging from the statistical evidence, though, the most dangerous thing in the world would be to operate a peevish vending machine on a golf course with your left hand during a thunder storm while thinking about having sex with an old man in a silver car.

Maybe that's not the most dangerous thing in the world though. Maybe the most dangerous thing in the world is to pay too much attention to statistics.

Statistics are the new superstition. There is truth in them, but they should not become the truth in themselves. Where are the statistics for talent, flair and instinct? What about pride, heart and soul? Where are those statistics? Can everything in life really be reduced down to basic numeric values? And if so, will statistics really provide the answers to all of life's great mysteries?

Sometimes I'm just not sure that I want to know. With all due reverence to the geeky fanboy/girl lurking inside every one of us (you know its there – that tiny part of you that can recite, in order, the last ten celebrity Big Brother evictees, that can accurately describe the style of every Wigan strip of the last decade; that part of you that knows what a bandril looks like – it is the part of you that thinks it can justify stalking) sometimes I feel that focussing on the numbers takes some of the magic away. Call me old fashioned if you will, but there are times – mainly when Wigan win – when I just want to enjoy the experience. My team won. That's it. We won and we won because we're Wigan and our players are wonderful (or, at the very least, better than theirs) and all is right with the world.

That's a great feeling to have. It is truly joyous. The last thing I want is then to have pundits like Paul Cullen telling me that had their left centre not dropped his right shoulder by two inches, he would have been able to make the tackle, preventing the try and causing us to lose. Or that the victory came as a result of the opposite team adopting a man-on-man marking system and then switching to a sliding defence for some inexplicable reason. No! I want to think that we won because we're great and for no reason other than that.

Ok, so I might be guilty of burying my head in the sand, but I like to think that sometimes the world is not entirely governed by strict physical laws and, more importantly, that good teams sometimes win just because they're good. Is that so unreasonable?

Possibly it is. Nevertheless, I don't always want our victories rationalised to the Nth degree. Apart from anything, else, it seems to be contrary to the spirit of the game.

I remember once laughing out loud as an email from a supporter of Leeds (I think) was read out on Boots'N'All.

The email was criticising Tony Rea for his post match analysis of a previous Leeds game which, according to this enraged viewer, had shown all the other teams in Super League the best way to beat Leeds.

"What a muppet!" I remember thinking. It would be unthinkable that a Boots'N'All analyst would be giving away tactical information that any other Super League coach wouldn't already have worked out for himself. And I think it's reasonable to say that if your head coach is relying on Boots'N'All as his primary source for game tactics then you can probably resign yourself to a fairly mediocre season.

In some ways, though, that rather desperate and deranged Leeds supporter might have had a point. What business do Tony Rea, Paul Cullen et al have spoiling the wonderment of the whole thing? If, for instance, I had been attending a live magic show and then, having enjoyed that magic show so much – the silver hoops, the flaming swords and the sparkly tights – I felt moved to watch a further programme based upon that show ("Hoops'N'All", perhaps), then I'm sure that having the magic equivalent of Paul Cullen appear and tell me exactly how the tricks are done, it would spoil some of my appreciation of it.

Throughout my job I am a slave to data. The stream of numbers and grades and achievement margins is relentless. Baseline data informs target levels to be continually assessed against local factors, all of which are then collated to create rich intervention strategies which hopefully result in meaningful outcomes that become the next set of baseline data. Then it starts all over again. And none of this is bad. I'm all for the use of data and empirical evidence to effect improvement in my job. But ONLY in my job.

What I don't want to do is then go and apply the same data-centric approach to my private and personal life. The thought of the ensuing conversations with Mrs Macaulay makes my blood run cold. The balance of picking my clothes up off the floor combined with meaningful conversation and relinquishment of the remote control against time spent in the pub and attending rugby games would not look good on paper. I have a nasty feeling that the data would prove me to be a failing husband and father. I'd be put in special measures for sure. The pressure would be too much and my performance would suffer as a result.

Sometimes too much scrutiny and data can be a very negative tool.

It can distract you from your goals in favour of an overly-analytical approach to the process by which you might achieve those goals. A bit like taking your eye off the ball while you correctly align your hands prior to making the catch. The result? Great poise, but still a knock-on.

Moreover, it can sully the truly enjoyable bits of life by seeking to impose unrealistic ways of measuring them. For instance, supporters are there to enjoy the game. How do you quantify enjoyment? We don't naturally speak of enjoying the game to a numerical value. We express such matters in non-quantitive phrases such as "that was a bloody good game!" And that should be enough.

Yet Boots'N'All wouldn't broadcast detailed match analysis without their being a big enough audience for such material. This means there is a sizeable contingent of fans who not only enjoy statistics, but thrive on them.

Perhaps this isn't too hard to believe. There is, after all, an accountant lurking within each one of us. In my case, though, he's lurking so deep inside that I'm rarely troubled by him. I'm not all that keen on numbers, to be honest, but even I can appreciate that a mastery of numbers and data can make people seem quite knowledgeable and impressive. It is a means of educating oneself to a level where people will think your views are important. I recently read that the Greeks claim to have invented maths. This is difficult to accept, bearing in mind their country's current financial predicament. It would be like Italians claiming they invented credible politicians.

Actually, the Greeks claim to have invented democracy too. Again, the pinch of salt rule applies. But even if they did invent maths and democracy, you shouldn't be drawn into thinking that they have always had the intellectual Midas touch. Some of their most eminent philosophers were about as credible as Italian politicians. Diogenes would spend his days sat in a barrel and playing with himself, Plato basically made his reputation out of inventing shadow-puppet theatre and Socrates was just an awkward old bugger who would argue that black was white just for the opportunity to wind people up. They poisoned him, eventually.

So while some people like to feel that the association between mathematical expertise and intelligence is on a rock solid foundation, it should always be remembered that mathematical excellence is also associated with shadow puppets and masturbating in barrels.

Suddenly the statisticians don't seem quite so impressive, do they? And be honest, who would you rather spend the evening with – your mates or a pocket calculator? Maybe they are one and the same. Perhaps some of us can actually find it worthwhile to strike up a meaningful relationship with a mechanism of statistics and data.

I remember a time in my early teenage years when I took my younger sister to see a movie at the local cinema. The film was called "Electric Dreams" and was basically about a man whose home computer fell in love with him. At the time the thought of a man striking up such a relationship with his computer was strikingly novel. Since then, of course, "doing the Diogenes" in front of your computer screen has become a worldwide phenomenon. Apparently. (One set of statistics tells me that eighty per cent of internet usage is the viewing of pornography). However, back in the day, I was intrigued at the prospect of having any kind of relationship with a machine. I only knew one family who had a home computer – The Mellings – and whenever we visited them I would creep[33]

---

33   "Creep" being the operative word.

into the darkened bedroom that housed the computer, close the door behind me and whisper sweet nothings into its vent while gently caressing its generously proportioned central processing unit. Sadly, we never quite hit it off. Mr Melling's computer didn't have the same gift for pleasing dialogue that made the computer in Electric Dreams so alluring. In fact the most romantic thing it ever said to me was "Abort, Retry, Fail" – words that at the time were meaningless but have since come to encapsulate every relationship I have ever had. I suppose I had a lucky escape. The alternative would have been a relationship based on binary codes. That's not real love. It's an attempt at love that misses the target. What Diogenes did in his barrel wasn't real love. It is pseudo-love for those who are too shallow for the real thing. The sort of love that insecure men have for their cars. It's Jeremy Clarkson love. Similarly, we may all know people who are overly fond statistics, but it is not a real relationship we have with them. It is a pseudo-relationship where the cloud of data they are orally dispersing distracts you from any real interaction. Real interaction is about feelings.

Therefore, it is my assertion that a love for data and statistics on the part of a rugby league fan is also a love that misses the real target. It is a love of numbers and of facts and of detail, all masquerading as a love of rugby league.

I am acutely aware that this view does not necessarily align me with the majority of rugby league fans[34]. In fact I

---

34 Although I have no stats to back this up.

now note that Phil Clarke's weekly dose of statistical data diagnostics has disappeared completely from Boots'N'All. Instead you can watch it as a red button optional extra. Eddie Hemmings cheerfully informs us that this is because it has become so incredibly popular. The cynic in me can't help but wonder why, if this is the case, Boots'N'All isn't the red button option? Nonetheless, Phil Clarke is now serving up the stats together with Brian Carney in their own show on Sky Sports. Even a numeracy-hating romanticist like myself couldn't resist the lure of two former Wigan greats analysing the weekly rounds and so I duly red buttoned myself in on it.

It was clear to me from the first minute that something had gone terribly wrong. Phil and Brian were in a state of medical crisis. The numbers had got to them. It can happen to any man who spends too much time perusing figures – Datadelirium! There they were, all excited and sweaty-browed, rattling out facts and figures ten to the dozen, at speeds that the human mouth just wasn't designed for. It was unsettlingly like watching your old school maths teachers try to teach long division after some wag had spiked their coffees with weapons-grade amphetamines.

I looked on, aghast, as tackles, missed tackles, clean breaks and try-assists were fired from my TV set and ricocheted around my living room, courtesy of the two wild-eyed, over excited data maniacs. By the time the programme had finished I felt like I'd had my brain raped by the Numberjacks. And, as is the way with these red button affairs, no sooner had it finished and my number-numbed brain was beginning the recovery process, than the programme started again right from the very beginning. It took ten minutes with my head in a bucket of chopped onions just to get to a point where I could have a statisticless thought again. And did this experience leave me any more knowledgeable in the dark arts of rugby league? Did it even enhance my appreciation of the game?

In both cases, I'd have to concede that the answer was "no".

Despite this, many fans can (and frequently will) tell you straight away and without having to think too hard exactly what our pack's weight ratio and distribution is compared to that of the visiting team, and so on. While they might not be the most stimulating conversationalists in the stadium, there is no questioning their zeal for the statistics. They will argue that rather than such data being a distraction, there is a further enjoyment to be gleaned from the memorising of statistical facts and figures and from an intimate understanding of tactical analysis. This is total-immersion-fandom. In their view it signifies the move from being an active supporter to becoming an obsessive and passionate devotee. It is a perfectly natural progression, and the supporters who follow this path can expect to benefit in many ways. Significantly, they get to feel like experts. This, they feel, will give them the right to broadcast their views to anybody who will or won't listen.

It may be the case that nobody agrees with them (in fact they rarely agree with each other) but that won't bother them. Why should it bother them? They are, after all, the experts – or so they'll tell you.

We all know supporters like this. And we've probably all been supporters like this. The truth is that we have all found ourselves sliding towards this end of the supporters spectrum at some point. But, like the Greeks, we should be wary of the pitfalls of such mathematical aggrandisement. It comes hand in hand with dodgy barrels and social bankruptcy – sooner or later people will start to call you "weird" or "tedious."

To be a real expert, of course, you have to take tedium to a whole new level. Your scrutiny of the tiniest details must be rigorous enough to pass the muster of an academic discipline at the highest level. This will almost certainly entail the sort of meticulous analysis of mind-bendingly dull facts that would push your average computer to the brink of a nervous breakdown. It is to leap, whole-heartedly and smiling, into a world of torturous boredom. It makes you wonder just what sort of person would be willing to engage in such an activity.

I was interested to read that Phil Clarke chose to spend four months of his life looking at how, where, when and why all the one thousand five hundred and ninety tries were scored during the course of the 2009 Super League season. Together with Dr Bill Gerrard (a lecturer in Sports Science and a renowned expert in statistical performance analysis), he engaged himself in the rigorous and painstaking process of exhaustively identifying the patterns and trends of try scoring, before singling out the key factors in every single try scored.

It took them four whole months. I can't begin to imagine how painful that must have been. Truly, Mr Clarke has shown devotion to and expertise in the area of rugby league minutiae. My own personal idea of a comprehensive review of try scoring, is a few minutes of conversation over a couple of pints in the dingy corner of a local pub. Maybe with some helpful scribblings on a beer mat. But then, I am not tasking myself with the job of making significant advances in playing technique across the entire league. While it might be easy to mock the navel-gazing approach of the statisticians, if it proves to be the difference between victory and failure in the next world cup, then I will be the first in the queue to bow before them. Logic tells us that the time, effort and expense of such a job would almost certainly be rewarded with some clear, meaningful outcome on the pitch. At the very least, it must surely throw up some surprising, perhaps even shocking insights into our game that have eluded countless blokes in pubs defacing their beer mats.

With this in mind, I was eager to hear what the results of four months of full-on research might be. There were, as it transpired, some interesting findings brought to light by the endeavour. Phil Clarke lists his findings as follows:-

- Most tries are scored in the last ten minutes of each half.

- Teams with the best defensive record have a better chance of finishing high up in the table.
- 50% of tries are scored from close range.
- Teams that can attack well from between 11 and 40 metres from their opponents' try line tend to do well in the competition.
- Teams whose players are physically stronger than others are more successful, although they don't necessarily score tries that are dependent on strength.
- Teams that have to rely on kicking to score tries have a tendency to finish lower in the league table.
- The team that finished top that year (Leeds) were superior to other teams in their strength, their ability to off-load the ball and the number of long passes they used.
- Wigan were better than any other team at scoring tries that involved the creation and utilisation of space.

Curiously enough, I have exactly the same points scrawled on a beer mat round here somewhere. Although, to be fair to Phil Clarke, my spelling wasn't anywhere near as good.

To be less flippant, although the list contains some glaringly obvious points – the frequency of tries scored in the last ten minutes of each half, the importance of strength and the suggestion that tries scored from kicks are the tactics of less successful teams, to name a few – there are also some very interesting findings. Certainly there are some things there that are worth further consideration.

For instance, the fact that the more successful teams

are the ones who have greater attacking ability between 11 and 40 metres of their opponents' try line is an intriguing point. The notion that rugby league is all about camping on your opponent's try line and plugging away until you manage to crash over (something that I often hear as a criticism of the game) is exposed here as a misnomer. I can't honestly say that this piece of information comes as a shock. It was something that I had always suspected, or maybe just assumed. It stands to reason that a team who need to be camped on your try line in order to score tries can be beaten by being starved of territory. A team who can score from further away are significantly more dangerous. This correlates nicely with the information gleaned about the impact that a team's physical strength has on their success and the scoring of tries. Yes, physically stronger teams fare better in the league table. But the figures also tell us that those teams do not rely on their strength to score tries. Presumably strength works to their advantage defensively, or in ensuring dominance and maximum impact when running into the tackle, driving defenders back and keeping the opposition on the back foot. This in turn creates space and time for creativity and the further exploitation of space in that 11-40 metre area. Every rugby league spectator knows that your pack "creates the platform" for your backs. These statistics certainly serve to rationalise and to elaborate on the maxim. Again, though, it's hardly rocket science. Taken in isolation, any of the findings make the survey seem trivial. It is when you start linking them together that they begin to enhance your understanding of the game. The holistic view will always be the most revealing view. If nothing else, it is nice to see that the facts and figures serve to underline what we all thought we knew anyway. It is also reassuring to know that studies of such depth are being undertaken, and that a team like Wigan is keen to take note of the findings. In the quest for success no stone should be left unturned. And while you might argue that it isn't rocket science, a bit of orbital satellite surveillance science surely wouldn't go amiss.

Recently the club invested in a state of the art GPS tracking system that enables the coaching staff to keep accurate records of every single step players make on the pitch. Recalling a game played a few years ago at Odsal in dense fog, I immediately saw some sense in the idea. At least on a night like that one, GPS trackers would mean that somebody somewhere would have some idea what was going on. Initially I thought it was a system designed to allow the coach to stand on the touchline with a megaphone shouting directions at fog-blinded players. After giving it some thought, though, my general mistrust of technology and data began to gnaw at me. Why spend bucket loads of money on 007 gadgetry when, by simply placing a bell around each player's neck, you can achieve a similar result for a fraction of the price.

Here is my sensible, cost-cutting solution for those nights when Sky insist that games are played regardless of conditions. When those in attendance are treated to zero-visibility rugby league. And when those watching from the comfort of their homes might be forgiven for thinking that they've accidentally tuned in to a Stephen King film – can you imagine what the image of Jamie Peacock suddenly looming out of the murk must look like to the casual viewer? In 2010 a notorious fog-shrouded clash between St Helens and Hull FC was one of the highest rating TV events of the month, picking up not only the faithful rugby league viewers, but also several thousand soccer fans, who just weren't quite sure that they weren't watching football, and a dark legion of horror aficionados who described the event as the most terrifying thing they had ever seen on TV before the watershed.

In my view, a clever combination of campanology and common sense can salvage a foggy game and ensure an enjoyable evening. Each player is given a small bell to be hung around his neck. The bells for each team are of a different tone – bass and tenor, let's say. They can incorporate this into the toss for kick off – the team that loses the toss gets the consolation of being able to choose between deep resonating bongs or tinkling fairy bells. Each player's bell chimes a different note, dependant on their position. That way you know who you are passing to. The referee is equipped with a horn which he must honk periodically in order to enable players to ascertain his position on the pitch at all times (you wouldn't want any harm to "accidentally" come to him in that thick fog).

Extra points can be awarded for the team that puts together the most tuneful attacking move that leads to a try.

DING DING DONG DING DONG DONG
DING
HONK HONK!
WHISTLE!

It makes a high-tech GPS player tracking system seem not only unnecessary but also musically dull, doesn't it?

But then, I speak only as a mere fan who likes to believe that life should come complete with its own accompanying soundtrack. Even if it is just honks and bells.

To the master statistician, sitting in his lair of numbers and fondly stroking his Spearman's Rank Index, the tracking system cultivates a whole new, fertile field of number-related crops to harvest. You can literally see every movement a player makes – every step of every run made in attack or defence. This enables you to ascertain which players are wasting their energies on unnecessary exertions and which ones aren't quite getting to where they need to be. It is indeed a very powerful tool.

There is definitely a place for numbers and figures and graphs and the like in our game, but where should that place be? Every rugby mad fanatic wants to be able to back up his or her pet theories with some good, hard facts. Just like the Daily Mail likes to corroborate its outlandishly sensationalised middle-England-centric flights of fancy with some roughly honed suggestion of what the truth might possibly be if you squint at it long enough through a glass of Rioja. We all want the security of hard facts to underpin our faith. Then again, many rugby fans would agree that there is much to be said for just being able to lose yourself in the magic and joyful amazement of watching a game when sometimes your team wins and sometimes it doesn't.

Somewhere there must be a happy medium. Like Mystic Meg – she seems to be a happy medium. At least, she does once you get past her tendency to read your fortune in the same way a divorce lawyer might explain your settlement.

"Pisces – you have an expensive month on the cards…"

Yes, Mystic Meg will be the one to break the worst possible news imaginable, but she will always do so with an enigmatic smile on her face. Either she enjoys delivering bad news, or there is some deep and profound effect that communing with the spirit world has upon a menopausal woman with a paganism fixation. Either way, she is a happy medium. And her many followers are happy too, because while she delivers the bad news, everybody knows that it has absolutely no factual basis. Mystic Meg can't really predict the future. People are fine with that. They just enjoy the smoke and the mirrors and the show. They enjoy it in a way that you don't enjoy discussions with your divorce lawyer. Mystic Meg is proof that we like to be entertained, and we can be entertained without requiring any factual information.

What happens, though, when a sports broadcasting company derails itself from the track of entertainment in order to become immersed in data delirium? I will tell you. The margin meter happens. The margin meter was a mercifully short lived innovation. It gobbled up raw data, pondered the variables and from the resultant calculations it extrapolated the course of upcoming events. Basically, in the margin meter, Sky Sports had invented a machine that predicted the future. It succeeded where even Mystic Meg had failed.

Take a moment to think about this. It represents an astounding technological advancement with enormous repercussions for the entire human race. And we used it to tell us what the final score of Super League matches was going to be.

Sky Sports did this during the games themselves. Not via the red button or on a special website for die hard rugby league addicts. No, the thing was emblazoned across the screen as the action unfolded in the background. Imagine being a neutral viewer tuning in to the sport for the first time. Just as you're getting excited about the way the game is progressing, somebody flashes up the final score for you. It is the televised sporting equivalent of somebody handing you a carefully wrapped and curiously shaped Christmas present and, as they do so, saying "it's a cake stand."

The rug of anticipation is pulled from under your feet. Why bother watching anymore? You might as well switch channels and watch another sport that might be less exhilarating in its execution but at least retains that all-important sense of mystery for as long as possible.

The margin meter embodied the inescapable and

ultimately depressing result of following the path of statistical data analysis to its definitive conclusion. Number crunching inevitably robs you of enjoyment. Yes, there is a certain amount of satisfaction to be gleaned by a certain type of people from such an exercise. I can see that. Unlocking the mysteries of rugby league using data can feel both reassuring and empowering. I'm happy for coaches, bookies and pundits to have this data, to scrutinise it and to use their findings to further their various causes. I'm happy for the viewing public to be party to the facts and the processes whereby the tackles, busts, assists, use of substitutions, kicks in general play and location and speed of the play the balls influence the result of the game. That's all great. But not thrown in your face as a fait accompli while you're watching the game itself. Because this means your love of the statistics and the data and the numbers has overtaken your love of the game itself. When that happens, you lose sight of the real joy in the life – the magic of the moment.

The statisticians among the movers and the shakers at Sky Sports fell into this very trap and the margin meter was the result. Entertainment took a back seat as we followed the numbers. This is almost the exact opposite of what rugby league should be about. Our game is built on the notion of providing entertainment to a paying public. Our game is shunt and grunt, big hits, high octane power and flair and style. It's not a sport that deserves to be chained up and shackled by the crunching of numbers. And if the margin meter really had been all that good at predicting the future then it should've realised right from the outset that its days were numbered.

Statistics may or may not be misleading. It probably depends on who you are and what you're doing with them. They can certainly be confusing and can be used to support any argument you wish to propose. They might even be quite enjoyable in their own right. But they're not rugby league – they'll never be that enjoyable.

They are the brown sauce on your pie. On its own, brown sauce isn't something anybody in his right mind would admit to enjoying. You don't go round to your mate's house for an evening of brown sauce. That's disgusting. Even Diogenes didn't do that.

Brown sauce, however, when added to your pie as an accompaniment, enhances the flavour and thus the enjoyment of said pie. This is the beauty of the brown sauce. It is why we are drawn to it. We all know that the pie is real star, though, and at heart we deeply mistrust those who ask for a pie to accompany their brown sauce.

Statistics are the saucy accompaniment to the pie that is rugby league. If we want to retain what is really good for our game then pie must always come first

Rugby league as a concept is what should always come first and foremost in our hearts and minds. It is the pie. Statistics might well enhance our enjoyment of rugby, but at what price?

We all have our favourite teams and our favourite players. Do we choose our favourite teams on the basis of statistical evidence? Of course not. We choose them on the basis of emotional attachment and of conceits. We think we are the best because we love Wigan. Similarly, why do we love our favourite players? It rarely has anything to do with statistical evidence. There is just something about them that chimes with us. I didn't have such warm regard for Sam Panapa as a result of counting his tackles, line breaks and try assists. There was just something about him that I liked and found entertaining. I could probably say the same about Martin Foy and countless others. In my mind they were great players. Statistics may say otherwise. Statistics may even accuse my judgements of such players of being lies. I don't care. In my mind the brown sauce has its place and it should remember its place. Pies, damned lies and then statistics.

GRAND FINALE

"The End Is Nigh."

The first time I saw those words was on a sandwich board worn by a strange man who used to hang around Central Park on Sunday afternoons prior to kick off. He perplexed me. In fact he used to single out my father for particularly special treatment.

"You should know better, father," he said in his smug yet desperate way. Not only did my infant mind have to grapple with the concept of humanity's impending doom, but also with the use of the word "father" by somebody who was clearly older than my dad himself.

As my father led me quickly to the turnstiles, my hand safely enclosed in his, the inquisitive nature of the very young got the better of me.

"Who was that?" I asked, knowing full well – as did my father – that my question wasn't just one pertaining to the identity of this strange old gentleman who claimed to be my impossible brother. It was also a question about the truth of our inevitable and impending end; about the fleeting nature of existence itself and about the apparent contrast between the sense of security instilled by the presence of my father and the fear brought about by this stranger's ominous remonstrations.

"Well," said my dad in his endlessly loving and affable manner, "he's just a bloody nutter."

The sandwich board man became a regular fixture of my youthful Sunday afternoons. Regardless of his sanity or intent, he was the instigator of my first thoughts about the finality of everything.

The cat was out of the bag. I now knew that all things had to end and it occurred to me that endings must be of particular importance.

There was another expression I'd heard:-

"All is well that ends well".

I'm not sure where I was or how old I was when I first heard this said, but I know that it also seemed to make sense to me. Again, it stressed the importance of the ending – the component that provides meaning and integrity to the rest of the journey.

A good ending is vital – rugby league has always told me this. With this in mind, how does rugby league approach "the end"? How have we chosen to wrap up and finish off a season-long campaign of scintillating rugby league?

I'll tell you – up until very recently we have done it like this.

First plays fourth, second plays third. Fifth plays eighth and sixth plays seventh. The loser of the first versus fourth then plays the winner of the fifth versus eighth. And the loser of the second versus third plays the winner of the sixth versus seventh.

Then the winner of the first versus fourth plays the winner of the loser of the first versus fourth versus the winner of the fifth versus the eighth. And the winner of the second versus the third plays the winner of the loser of the second versus third versus the winner of the sixth versus seventh. Unless, that is, the highest placed winner of the first versus the fourth and the second versus the third doesn't fancy doing it this way round. In which case they'll do it the other way round. And the winning two teams will then face each other in the Grand Final at Old Trafford.

This is the model of the most recent play-off system. Of course, it's all about to change, but up to October 2014 this is how we've been doing things. It has been like a heady combination of algebra, snakes and ladders, Pop Idol, Russian Roulette, British Bulldog, and Twister. And somebody at RLHQ thought this up and decided that it would be the ideal way to end the Super League season. It was their response to "the end is nigh." Fortunately, though, we are now due to be propelled into the new era with a radically different season structure. Each team will play twenty four league games prior to the "Super Eights". At the ringing of a bell the respective league tables will be carved into groups of eight based on league position. Each group of eight will then play a mini-league to determine final league positions. The top four teams in Super League will then play off in order to reach the Grand Final. While it may well be simpler than the previous format, it still gives me a headache just thinking about it.

The big question here is really this: regardless of the format of the play-off structure, is a play-off tournament really a better way to end the season than the old fashioned "first-past-the-post" system?

For those of us who are to mathematics what Shaun Wane is to Flamenco Dancing[35], then the play-off competition serves just to add a little more stress and confusion to the end of the season. It used to be confusing enough as it was. I had just about got my head around the old fashioned league table system, with its two for a win, one for a draw and none for a lose, combined with points difference. That's the way things were before we started "playing off with ourselves." It was certainly more than complicated enough for my liking but at least you knew that the outcome was clear. The most consistent team won the league.

Admittedly, more often than not, as the end approached, you would find yourself having to figure out not only how many matches Wigan would have to win or draw, but also how many tries we would have to win by.

At the same time you would be desperately doing the same frenzied calculations for all of our near rivals, just to ensure that they didn't sneak up on you while you were playing with your abacus.

There may well be some truth in the sneering

---

35 This is just based on a rumour I have heard, but the image it
    creates in my head is endlessly entertaining.

allegations that there were seasons during Wigan's period of dominance when the sums would say "we need to win one of our last eight games by three points and not lose the others by over four hundred points, while Leeds need to win twelve of their last eight by an average margin of two hundred thousand points per game just to draw level."

But the fact of our enduring success coupled with the satisfactory nature of the result did little to detract from the difficulty and pain of having to do such complex mathematics in the first place. I know of leading city bankers who couldn't do sums like that (at least, they *were* leading city bankers, but since the collapse of Lehman Brothers and the ensuing global financial meltdown, for the most part they are now in hiding).

If what you're after is fair reward with a bit of complexity and a few sums thrown in, then the first past the post system was fine.

But, in some darkened lair deep in the vaults of Sky TV HQ, someone was doing sums of different kind. They were doing bums sums (or bums-on-seats sums to give them their official title). And their calculations pointed to the fact that by denying the best team of the entire season their right to a reward, effectively you could keep the clenched bums of the supporters of all the other teams glued to their seats.

And so the play-offs were born. Or rather, they were pinched lock, stock and barrel from our antipodean counterparts. And why not? We'd already pinched Kylie, barbeque cuisine and the high rising terminal inflection from right under their noses. What would it matter if we nicked the play off system too?

The Australians, of course, are never ones to let another nation get the better of them and it would appear that they have chosen to take their revenge by inflicting Stevo upon us in a cruel sort of time-share arrangement. And yet still some people think the play offs are worth it.

As a means of concluding the rugby league season, the play offs have been not only mathematically mind-boggling, but they also represent a significant threat to the value of the regular season. Consider that at the culmination of the 2012 regular season, Wigan finished top of the league table. The team were duly handed the League Leader's shield and a bit of a fuss was made. Not much of a fuss, mind. A couple of over-sized party poppers and a few photographs of the players holding up the plate.

If you look at those photographs, you can see that the players are smiling. But look beyond the smiles. Gaze deep into the eyes of those plate-waving players and you will see a complete absence of rapture. There is no joy there, none of the explosive exultation that you might normally associate with true celebration. Instead there is just a haunting emptiness. That, and the sense of worry and fear of those who feel conspicuous about celebrating a job half-done. Similarly, the celebration of the on-looking supporters is guarded and hesitant. I know this because I was there.

It was exactly the same way that my grandparents

cheered when they were teaching me to ride my bike without stabilisers for the first time. They cheered because I had successfully managed to cycle upright with minimal wobbleage on a down-hill stretch. But it was only a half-hearted cheer because they knew full well that the hill was about to get much steeper with a busy crossing awaiting me at the bottom. While I had indeed achieved something, there was still ample opportunity for disaster.

Is this really the fitting way to mark the culmination of the regular season? Should the team that shows the most consistency throughout the seemingly endless onslaught of demanding fixtures really be rewarded with a half-hearted, perfunctory, muffled cheer? Is this how we want our regular season to end – not with a bang but with a whimper? If you ask me, it didn't ever seem entirely fitting. We still have the bang, of course, but that is reserved for the winners of the play off games. The feat of being the most consistent team is rewarded with the whimper.

I would even go as far as to say that those supporters who claim that the regular season had been reduced to the level of a series of pre-season friendlies have got a very strong argument. I don't entirely agree with them, though. Apart from anything else, I happen to enjoy the "sturm und drang" of the regular season. In fact I actually enjoy rugby. I will watch rugby for rugby's sake rather than watching purely in the hope of seeing success or silverware. I find success and wonderment and joie de vivre in a well-executed set move, or in a bit of spontaneous free-flowing ball play or in an amazing defensive effort. For me, these are the real, life-affirming moments delivered on a weekly basis by my favourite game.

Each seasonal campaign provides us with moments of triumph and heart-break. We see exhilarating rugby from our team and from other teams. We laugh together in the stands and after we've left we will grumble over the errors, mistakes and missed opportunities until the bell for last orders rings in our ears. No matter what convoluted system the RFL imposes on the business end of the season, none of this will change.

Nevertheless, the nature of the competition (prior to 2015) did give rise to a number of deep and philosophical questions regarding tactics.

Should a discerning coach treat every game throughout the season as a final in its own right and go hell for leather from the outset, trying to win them all? Or is it better to keep a little back? To pace yourself and then give it all you've got as you go into the play offs? In other words, should the Super League season be a sprint or a marathon?

Leeds, of course, managed to turn the business of losing more regular season games than necessary and then beating all comers in the play offs into a veritable art form. If I'm honest, I don't think they have ever planned it that way. Whereas Warrington definitely did. Their coach continuously rested and rotated his players throughout the year, choosing his battles with the utmost care. To his credit, the result has been some entertaining displays of rugby league football by visibly fresh players in the games where it really mattered.

By contrast, at the start of his tenure, Wigan's current coach set his stall out from day one. He wanted to win them all – every single game. He wanted all three trophies and he wanted the world to know he was going to take it on. The very thought still sends shivers of excitement running up and down my spine. I applauded this attitude.

It wasn't just the honesty. Nor was it the implicit respect shown to all opposition. It wasn't even the sheer ambition of the mission statement. It was the appreciation of who and what we are. We are Wigan, the world famous rugby club. We compete. We do so in every possible capacity. Place an obstacle before us and it is our sworn duty to put everything we have into overcoming it. Put a team in front of us and we are honour-bound to beat that team. We do so by fielding our best available players and by treating the opposition to a bit of our style and flair (having first pummeled them senseless with some magnificent forward play). It is shock and awe in cherry and white. It is the Wigan Way. It is who we are and it is what we do. We won't win them all – of course we won't. But where's the harm in trying?

I never liked the implication of treating weaker teams differently. That isn't respecting them, it is the quite the opposite. Similarly, to say "we can afford to lose this one" is to disrespect the loyal, paying supporters who turn up to watch.

In Shaun Wane's first season as head coach, Wigan finished top of the league. We may not have won the competition, but it was more than good enough for me. I know there were those who disagreed with me. They pointed out, perhaps with good reason, that this tactic left our key players tired and less effective at the conclusion of the season. Even if this was the case, I didn't actually care. I am a man of principle. It might well be that this approach did leave us with injures and a drained team when it really mattered. It might be the case that we fell at the final hurdle. But to the critics I quote Mal Reynolds' response after he was queried about his allegiances:

"May have been the losing side. Still not convinced it was the wrong one."

Besides, why worry about tired players? We are not a team, or even a squad. We are a club. As David Cameron famously released on the instruction of his PR gurus – "we are in this together." The difference is, at Wigan we actually mean it. Every individual working at every level within the club is there to be called upon to do his or her bit. When the call to arms comes, our younger, less experienced players must rise to the challenge and as supporters we must put our trust in them.

The fairy tale ending may elude us, but providing the desire and the sense of common purpose is there, then it won't do forever.

This was a philosophy that I wholeheartedly approved of. The alternative approach, as demonstrated by Shaun Wane following our failure to reach the 2012 Grand

Final[36], also had its merits. By picking and choosing his battles, the coach had the opportunity to "blood" younger players in games where the stakes weren't quite as high. Win or lose, we all love to see those youngsters coming through.

The result, of course, was that in 2013 Wigan walked away with both the Challenge Cup and the Super League Trophy. For me it was a tricky one – a matter of personal values versus a greater chance of success. I didn't let it worry me too much, though.

The criticism that has already been thrown at the new, upcoming league and play-off format is that it means teams will be unable to risk throwing rookies into the mix. Every game is potentially going to be more meaningful. What a brave choice for a sport to make! I say this with no hint of sarcasm or snide. We have sacrificed some of our sacred cows. We have shunned the license system that I loved (and that I still feel would have worked, with the help of Columbo) and we have boldly gone where no sport I know of has gone before. I have issues with relegation and the welfare of players and their families – they are issues that reach back to the reasons we went professional and separated ourselves from the RFU in the first place. However, it seems that the latest influx of Sky money will be instrumental in supporting the teams in lower leagues.

---

36 In truth it might not have been a tactical approach as much as it was a result of suspensions and injuries, but allow me to use it as an argument.

It could well prove to be a masterstroke. Each and every game will be imbued with real importance. But could it be true that this will seriously limit the opportunities for younger players to be introduced into Super League games?

It doubt it. If the dream is to come true and we see a league where every game is a full-on dogfight to the death, then the added and prolonged intensity will inevitably result in more injuries. The youngsters will still get their chances. In fact we might have to rely on the depth of the squad to a far greater degree than we ever have done.

Besides, youngsters always get to play. Can anybody honestly say to me that our team in the 2014 Magic game versus Leeds looked so youthful simply because it wasn't considered by Shaun Wane to be a high-stakes game? No? I thought not.

People are also concerned that Wigan will suffer in a high intensity competition. Those niggling past defeats to lower placed teams are cited as evidence that we just don't have the consistency.

This is a silly argument. All teams always raise their game against Wigan. They look on their fixture list and earmark the Wigan game as a "must-win" encounter. For many teams, and for their supporters, a win against the Warriors is almost as good as a Grand Final win. If the "new era" is successful and every game for every team does become a "must-win" match, then this will work in our favour. It will nullify the "Oh, look – its Wigan!" effect. And those teams who have always played the system, rotating players and choosing their battles, will find themselves having to adapt. If you've got an ageing squad, you're in trouble. We really will be "all in it together". I suspect, though, that the depth of Wigan's squad and the proliferation of youthful talent therein will ensure that, come the play-offs, we're in the mix. But who knows? A new era is a step into unchartered territory and another reason why rugby league is so compelling.

Despite appearances to the contrary, I have never actually been pregnant. I've done the next best thing, though – I've stood at the business end and mumbled inadequately as my wife gave birth to our children. Occasionally women try to attain some sort of moral victory over men by pointing out that men like me[37] don't have to go through the hell that is child birth. However, it did recently occur to me that the Super League play-offs are at the very least comparable to child birth, if not a little bit worse. I think it is the sense of expectation that does it. That, and the months of waiting, full of worry and anxiety. The feeling of being helplessly carried along in the wake of events you can't control. Then just as things seem to be coming to a head, you've got to give one final, almighty push to achieve your goal. It can be a turbulent, tumultuous period where normal life takes a back seat. It divorces you from the real world. This is another by-product of

---

37   And probably most other types of men, come to think of it.

the play-offs. They make everything else that is going on in the rest of the world seem inconsequential.

For instance, one of the real advantages of the play-off system for school teachers is that it gives them something more important than going back to school to worry about. I speak with some authority on this matter. Under normal circumstances the end of the summer holidays would be a time of dread and fear. However, when Wigan are in the play offs, I can look beyond the first day of term to the weekend after it. I can focus on what is really important. The play-off series of matches comes at just the right time of year to provide a much needed sense of perspective. Who cares what your line manager is screaming at you upon the start of the new academic year when there is a monster of a rugby league match just around the corner?

Meanwhile, out in the real world, the weather is changing.

In as clear a case of prophetic fallacy as I can think of, the meteorological forces are setting the tone for the games ahead. The end is nigh. The countdown to the final battle has begun. The days grow shorter, storm clouds muster angrily overhead, howling winds endlessly chase their own tails around our stadia, and generally it piddles down all over the Grand Final at Old Trafford.

It is certainly not the sunny festival that is the Challenge Cup final at Wembley. Not that we should complain, mind you. The bad weather compliments the whole ethos of the event perfectly. This is, after all, the taut and tumultuous climax to a campaign of mounting pressure. All that pent up energy is seeking a release. From a fan's perspective, the Grand Final is nothing short of a cloud burst of torrential proportions. It is an emotional explosion.

Such a momentous event can do strange things to a person. It churns you up. All supporters know this. It can take a real toll on you emotionally. The effect on players must be equally powerful, if not more so. The Grand Final is an event that exposes the human being that we supporters conveniently edit out of our assessment of a player's performance in other matches. That image of the dear departed Terry Newton crying his heart out at the final hooter being a case in point. It was a scene that was hungrily lapped up by the Sky Sports cameras. Whether it be through the tears of a hooker, or through an uncharacteristic moment of hot-headed lunacy from a form prop, the Grand Final is an arena that reminds us that our heroes are real people. They have all the vulnerabilities, raw emotions and susceptibilities that accompany humanity. The final game of the season is a crucible in which we burn away all irrelevancies until we are left with something pure. In this way the Grand Final has succeeded in providing documentary evidence of the honesty and nobility of our game. It reveals the endeavours of men who work hard to achieve their dreams and who wear their hearts on their sleeves.

Back in 2003, many supporters of other teams took the opportunity to mock Terry Newton's tearful outburst. But I salute him still. It was a tragic and bitter loss, and I took it as hard as anyone. I was distraught. Yet I couldn't find the bravery to show my feelings to the opposition supporters in the stand around me. Shamefully, I slapped on a smile and pretended it didn't matter. It takes a lot to lay your disappointment bare for all to see like Terry did. It shows the sort of integrity that other sports, sullied as they are by ball-tampering, match fixing and pantomime theatrics with fake blood capsules, would sweat (real) blood for. The Grand Final brings our greatest assets into sharp focus. And one of those assets is the inherent honesty of our game.

In Wigan's most recent Grand Final performance we witnessed the astonishing sight of Ben Flower punching a prone Lance Hohaia. While I could never and would never condone such an assault, again it was a demonstration of the sheer weight of pressure and expectation that these young men are performing under.

And it made the news headlines. Everybody was talking about it. Granted, most of the discourse was negative, but isn't it true that no publicity is bad publicity? Ben Flower's punch didn't just disappoint me, it devastated me. It left me heartbroken and numb. I was pleased that proportionate punishments were meted out by both the club and the Rugby Football League.

Do I forgive him? Or course I do.

Did it bring the sport into disrepute? No.

Taken on its own, served up cold and in slow motion, it is a horrendous act. There is no doubt about that. But it did serve as a reminder to the nation that rugby league is still alive and kicking and as passionate as ever. To bring the sport into disrepute requires more than a single, spontaneous act of violence on a rugby pitch. You might argue, I suppose, that it brings the player into disrepute. But there again, we all have our moments of madness, and how many of us are subjected to the demanding pressure cooker atmosphere of a Grand Final?

No event can ever be taken in isolation. There will be a process and Ben Flower will be nurtured through that process and helped to come to terms with his actions and his own personal heartbreak and disappointment. He will have tough times ahead, but he will be given the opportunity to repent and to make reparations. Hopefully the end result will be a man who is a better person and a more influential player.

So what does it take to bring a sport into disrepute? Simple – not affording a man such an opportunity. Cutting him loose, having put him in that position in the first place. Giving up on him. That would be disreputable.

I have mentioned two incidents, over ten years apart, that tell us something else about a Grand Final. It doesn't just provide us with a great game between two of the sport's finest teams. It provides us with moments that will be debated for years to come. Moments that are, in the eyes of Sky Sports, pure gold. In the hearts of those in attendance, the Grand Finals' golden moments are even more precious.

They are quite simply unmissable.

Which is why nobody should ever ask you to miss them.

I did have a friend once – a London chap called Andrew Naismith – who bestowed upon me the great honour of being Best Man at his wedding. I said "yes". Well, he was my friend, after all, and it was a particular honour to be chosen for such a role, especially given the fact that he chose me above his own brother. Such opportunities are few and far between for me. Unlike Andrew, I have no brothers who might feel compelled to ask me to fulfil this solemn role by virtue of birthright. And most of my close friends know me well enough to make me the very last person they would ask to be their Best Man. So this was a once in a lifetime opportunity that I would have been crazy to miss. I practically bit his hand off.

When I discovered that his wedding day clashed with the inaugural Super League Grand Final, I felt more like biting his head off. In the end it proved to be a most trying and difficult day.

Generally speaking, it is supposed to be the groom who is nervous on the big day. Sure enough, in keeping with the traditional Best Man job description, I happened to have a hip-flask full of nerve-calming "medicine" tucked up my sleeve. It wasn't for the groom, though. Poor Andrew never got a sniff of it. It was for me, and considering the state I was in, I required every last drop.

It still annoys me somewhat that Andrew had the audacity to glower at me the way he did during the episode we now refer to as "the temporary mislaying of the rings". He was supposed to be my mate. He would have known better than most that I had things on my mind that day. But that wasn't the only reason I was upset with him. What sort of a mad fool chooses a wedding venue, on Grand Final night, that doesn't even have a TV, let alone Sky Sports? It made no sense. So, in the event, I did what any half-decent Wigan fan would have done in such testing circumstances. That evening, as the rest of the wedding party and guests feasted in style, I was sat outside in the car with a bag of nuts and a can of bitter, tuned into BBC Radio 5 on the chauffeur's tinny radio, and taking regular phone calls and texts from my dad. Every so often the bride would stick her head out of the window and shout "Speech!" or "Toast!" or "Cutting Cake!" and I'd come rushing in looking slightly annoyed by the interruption. I'm told people like a Best Man's speech to be brief. Some people even like it extremely brief and delivered from the car park through an open window. I hope.

I haven't really seen or heard from Andrew since his wedding. Perhaps it is for the best. There is, though, a serious point to be made here. The introduction of the play off system and the Grand Final has created another date that has to be kept free. Another potentially "unmissable, must-see event" to build your schedule around. At least under the old reliable points system, if you had to miss the game in which the trophy was awarded, it didn't feel like it mattered too much. It was just one more game, and you could console yourself with the fact that you'd seen all the hard work done in all those other games you'd witnessed first-hand. Even on the rare occasions when the whole league table rested on the result of that final game, it still didn't feel like you were missing the greatest show on earth if you had to attend a wedding in London. By creating another do-or-die cup final, the RFL were in effect deliberately putting more pressure on the supporters. In particular, supporters relationships with their spouses come under more pressure. Your team may or may not be contesting the final and you may or may not know until the week before. Anybody who has to try to explain this to a wife whose feelings for the sport border on disdain will know the real meaning of pressure.

For some of us this added weight has the effect of ramping up the tension of the forthcoming final to dangerous levels.

What this means, in real terms, is that there is another annual opportunity for the strangest aspects of my personality to come to the fore. There is always a perceptible shift in my behaviour prior to a big game. In the lean years between 2003 and 2010, I was barely troubled by this affliction. But all those years without a Grand Final appearance to enjoy just served to exacerbate the problem. On the evening of Friday 1st October 2010, as Wigan's first Super League final appearance in seven years loomed on the horizon, my behaviour became conspicuously odd.

Living, as I do, one hundred and sixty miles away from the heartlands of rugby league, I knew that my tradition of drinking no fewer than four pints in a pub while wearing a replica shirt[38] and a hat[39] would at best raise a few inquisitive eyebrows. At worst, my behaviour might irritate the hordes of non-league types during what for them might otherwise have been an unremarkable evening out in their local pub. I was acutely aware of this as I pulled on my blue away shirt and pirate hat, prior to stepping out towards the nearest boozer. I was also acutely aware of the fact that my slavish devotion to traditions was getting the better of me. How would the hordes cope with this?

As it happened, I didn't have to worry too much about the hordes. I ended up sat alone in the disco, huddled in a dark corner where I had hoped to skulk in the shadows. I soon realised, though, that my skulking options were limited as I was intermittently lashed by fluorescent lasers and occasionally picked out by an array of revolving multi-coloured search lamps. So I sat alone and managed to get in a few quick skulks in the odd, sporadic moments that I wasn't bathed in disco light.

Just me, you understand.

I wasn't sitting alone in the sense of "I've not quite managed to lure a girl over here yet." I was sat alone in the sense of "there's no other bugger here but me." To be fair, the DJ was there too. He had just put the Vengaboys on,

---

38   The one that the team wouldn't be wearing the following day.

39   Any hat will do, but the curious powers of fate seem to dictate that the sillier the hat, the greater the chances of a Wigan win.

which probably went some way towards explaining why the place was so empty – that, and the fact that this was Ashton Keynes. If you're going to go dancing somewhere on a Friday night, Ashton Keynes isn't likely to be your first choice. Too many sheep, for one thing. They get under your feet on the dance floor. There are definitely some benefits to allowing the odd sheep into your local village pub-cum-nightclub. For example, at the end of the night you can roll them up and down the floor and what you are left with is basically alcoholic candy floss. If there is a better use for a sheep, then I'm yet to find it[40].

I digress. I was sat alone in my local pub as the Friday night disco was in full swing.

It was awkward. Me and the DJ (and the sheep), all trying not to exchange glances. He didn't want to acknowledge the fact that there was nobody here. I didn't want to acknowledge the fact that I was there. The sheep didn't want to acknowledge anything, preferring to mill about looking, erm…sheepish. So we all pretended not to see each other through the imaginary crowd on the dance floor. I was there by way of a tradition that I knew might well come to ignominious end on that very night. All it would take would be a St Helens victory the following day to free me of this frankly ridiculous, self-imposed superstition. I comforted myself with this thought as I sucked the foamy head off the top of my first pint of Wadworths 6X. That, I told myself, would be the

---

40   Then again, I'm not from Yorkshire.

silver lining on tomorrow's cloud. And suddenly I was languishing in despair again, which is difficult territory for a man whose usual temperament lies some way north of optimistic.

I just needed somebody to be there to say "Ah, don't worry – we're going to win!" A bit of camaraderie to bolster my constitution and ward off the nerves.

One pint gone.

The emotional and psychological effects of a Grand Final tends to creep on the supporter. Unlike with the Challenge Cup, the urgency and the desperation does not seem to present itself until fairly late in the day. It had hidden away somewhere in the dark recesses of my psyche and had then chosen to ambush me at the last minute in the village pub.

It became clear to me that I had to be strong. I was prepared to accept that defeat was nigh, but in the hours before the event it was up to me, and to me alone in this Leagueless corner of our green and pleasant land, to Keep The Faith. I raised my glass to the glory and honour of Wigan. I drank to the cause (albeit a lost cause). I saluted the team of players whose destiny was to take to the field the following day. I toasted the Ancient and Loyal borough.

Two pints gone.

I was beginning to feel the camaraderie stirring within me. My mobile 'phone was also stirring within my pocket; the gods of rugby had granted me that most sought after of holy grails – a Vodafone signal in Ashton

Keynes. I took the opportunity to text various members of my extended family. I did so seeking solace, affirmation and the strength that comes from numbers.

My mum was the first to text me back. Hers is the only 'phone I know that has a font specially designed to convey guilt and disappointment.

"HAVEN YOU BEEN DRINKS?" she had texted (she's not good with predictive texting). Now I was looking as sheepish as the pub's only other clientele. How did she know I "haven been drinks?" Does the woman have spies everywhere? I eyed the nearest sheep with overwrought suspicion.

Finally the message I had been craving arrived. My sister's husband had texted me back. He said he was confident. Suddenly, so was I.

Three pints gone.

Camaraderie was now alive and kicking and strutting its stuff on the dance floor of The Horse And Jockey in Ashton Keynes. The sound of Whigfield's "Saturday Night" that blared from the speakers was reduced to a background hum as I treated the gathering locals to all four verses of "Ancient And Loyal Upon My Chest."

Four pints gone. At this juncture I decided that the wisest thing to do would be to have a few more.

The following morning I woke up from a night of not sleeping. That's never good. It was six o'clock and an assortment of lucky underwear was already sitting on the radiator awaiting the parts of me that required lucky garments. "Why?" I asked myself in sleep-sodden state.

"Why do I single out my feet, genitalia and buttocks for the purposes of fortune? Why don't I have lucky cardigans or gloves?"

The answers didn't come and I abandoned the train of thought because I didn't like the station it was pulling in at. Instead I took some time to admire my new lucky pants. Technically they weren't lucky yet. They were new and devoid of luck, but the right result later that day would infuse them with fortune and status befitting winning pants. They would have all the greatness of my previous lucky pants, but with added gusset. Lovely.

Or, alternatively, they would become loser pants and would be relegated to the status of pants worn only when I happened to be suffering from chronic diarrhoea. And we'd see how long the gusset lasted then.

The morning of a Grand Final is a tense and disjointed affair. An exciting rugby match is better than any alarm clock I have ever owned and on an occasion such as this I was up and about just after dawn and bouncing around under the power of nervous energy.

Outside, my car was primed and ready, fully fuelled, spotlessly clean and sat on the drive at a rather awkward angle. It was, in fact, pointing directly at Old Trafford. I shuddered at the thought that I had done that on my return home from the pub the previous evening. It had seemed like a good idea at the time, and I have always got a handy compass knocking about the place. We are indeed fortunate that we have a wide driveway that is well off the public road. And that the neighbours were out.

As I dutifully obeyed my pre-match traditions and then set out on the journey to Old Trafford, this felt somehow different. It felt tumultuous and steeped in a haunting sense of dread. The end was nigh.

From the moment I gunned my Doblo's engine into life I had the distinct impression that for once I really knew my destination. I was heading to the terminus. This was the final journey. It really was the end.

For reasons I cannot fathom, the atmosphere at Old Trafford as both teams emerge from the tunnel does not quite match up to that of the walk out onto the pitch at Wembley. Perhaps there is something about Wembley that is hard-wired into the Wigan supporter's genetic coding. Nonetheless, the moment is till spectacularly awe-inspiring. It is both exhilarating and terrifying in equal measure. Half of me trembles with excitement while the other half trembles with fear.

In this sense it is very similar to the experience of losing one's virginity. In almost every other sense, though, it is markedly different. For instance, a drunken Saints supporter from the row above didn't jump on top of me as I lost my virginity. Nor were my parents stood alongside me gesticulating wildly throughout the proceedings[41]. But in both cases, the individual, trembling in dual excitement and fear, is lost in lust. The Grand Final induces a sense of tunnel vision and rugby-lust.

That blurred eighty minutes of intense heart-on-your

---

41 They're never there when you really need them, are they?

sleeve, fists in the air and lungs in your mouth action is what it is all about. In that heady and richly textured period of time, your senses are heightened and you are more than merely alive. You are a cherry-and-white furnace, burning at the heart of the universe. Everything else is peripheral. There is you, and the match, and the people around you, and anything beyond that pales into insignificance. This is your time in the spotlight and your time to be part of the most important event occurring in the entirety of all creation. Those exchanged glances, smiles and squeezed hands you share with friends, family and loved ones in this incredible environment are all the more special because of it.

The game itself will pull you this way and that, dragging you helplessly from one emotion to another like fish on a line. For better of for worse, you are hooked. And if it is for worse, then so what? At least you were there and you lived and breathed it. More importantly, you felt it resounding in your heart and in your soul. It is where you belonged and where you had to be.

When you are there, at the epicentre of an event of such seismic magnitude, the arguments against the play-offs and the Grand Final seem almost inconsequential. This is the end, and it is entirely fitting.

It all has to end somewhere – everything does. This is the nature of our fleeting existence; life is a sexually transmitted disease, and it's terminal. Sad as it may seem, a rugby season cannot simply continue indefinitely. The end must inevitably come, and in so doing it gives meaning to the whole season.

Death has always provided meaning to life, but we do not measure the worthiness of our lives by how we die. We measure it by how we choose to live. With this consideration, is it not more philosophically appealing to "live" our rugby season in a constant state of competition? It is, after all, the essence of sport. Without competition, what would be the point? The play-off system may be unpopular in some quarters, but it does provide the impetus, for most teams, to fight until the very end. It keeps alive the hope of glory that little bit longer, and where there is hope there is life.

I have to conclude that the old way – where your season could be over weeks before your final game – does not encapsulate the spirit I associate with Wigan Warriors Rugby League Football Club.

I love "never say die." I love "back from the brink". I love "against the odds". I love that glint in the seemingly defeated hero's eyes just before he turns the tables and wins the day. I love it when we strive and when we toil for glory, because that is when we are truly living. Not just in the play offs or the Grand Final. In every single game throughout the year. From the muddled and muddied chaos of pre-season friendlies, to the seat of the pants excitement of the Challenge Cup. From the fumbles and bungles of the earliest rounds to the stoic and steely defence of the final eliminator. Through every pass, kick, tackle, bust and clean break. Through every penalty, every pint and every pie. And when I am sat in WS6, Row S, Seat 160 that's when I feel truly alive.

Sat there alongside my father, in the town that is so special to me, I am part of a vibrant, exciting, living event. It is an event where every moment counts and it burns with the energy of endeavour and challenge. That's what life should be and it is how I want to live my life. If I do that then I know that when the end finally does come, I can face it without fear or regret.

Providing the end is not at the hands of St Helens.

Or Warrington.

Or Leeds.

CONCLUSION

Since I first put pen to paper on this pseudo-philosophical discourse I have in turn been sentimental, scathing, irreverent, precious, political, whimsical and very rarely philosophical.

My declared intent was to explore the Wigan fan's state of being. I was hoping to be able to put into words exactly what being a Warriors devotee means to me, while at the same time unearthing home truths that other fans would recognise.

Basically, I wanted it to be an evaluation worthy of the "osophy" suffix. I don't know how successful I have been in this, but I've got some fairly dark suspicions about it.

One thing has happened, though. I've had to think about it. I've had to look at my own behaviour and to consider what I do, how I go about it and what I do it for.

I now know that those bi-weekly phone calls to my dad in order to discuss team news aren't actually anything to do with rugby. They're just a reason to talk to my dad: to share something with him. We don't generally talk about how much we love each other. Obviously we don't – we're from Wigan. But we do discuss the merits and de-merits of playing a second row in the centres when injuries call for it. It amounts to pretty much the same thing, really.

Similarly, when people ask, as they sometimes do, why I feel that it is so important to follow the rugby, I now know the answer has got very little to do with rugby itself. It has rather more to do with all the other important rubbish that clutters my life. The government's educational reforms, the increasing cost of living, the welfare of my children, the on-going battles against illness undertaken by several people I dearly love – these are the really important things in my life.

The rugby is my release valve. Forty minutes each way when I don't have to worry about all that other stuff. Eighty minutes of excitement, tension, joy and despair to be experienced in a cauldron of noise. It provides the perfect opportunity to shout very, very loudly and get it all off my chest. Eighty cathartic minutes of pure theatre. It is important simply because it is an escape from all the other stressful paraphernalia of life.

I've held onto it. I'm barely recognisable as the nine year old lad who left Wigan never to return all those years ago. I've lived in so many different places since then that I'm not really from anywhere. Through Wigan Warriors RLFC, though, I have a touchstone that will always be a link to my roots.

Sadly, the day will come when those beloved relatives, who have always given me a sense of having come from somewhere, will be gone. I dread that day. But I do know that as long as I follow the Warriors – as long as I carry that season ticket in my wallet – I can walk round Wigan town centre and feel I have a spiritual home. I will always be a part of something.

Being anchored to your own past by something that will stand the test of time is important when you have vacated the stomping ground of your youth.

It is also something I can pass on to my children. They may or may not choose to follow the team as I have done, but that doesn't matter. What matters is that even when I'm dead and gone, every time the word "Wigan" is mentioned in the news, or is spotted on a sign post, they will think of me and of the principles I held dear. The past, I think, is the key to surviving the future.

So that's it. That's why I am a Wigan Warriors fan.

Well, that and the fact that they're clearly a great team who score the best tries in the most amazing fashion, but that's only to be expected. It is, after all, the Wigan Way.